COMPREHENSION AND GRAMMAR

PASCAL PRESS

CONTENTS

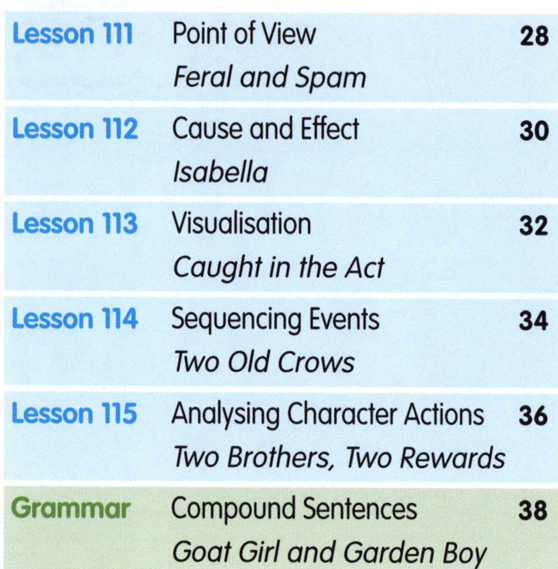

Term 1

Fiction Unit

Lexile Levels 780L–810L

Nonfiction Unit

Lexile Levels 790L–820L

Term 2

Fiction Unit

Lexile Levels 800L–840L

Nonfiction Unit

Lexile Levels 810L–840L

Term 3

Fiction Unit

Lexile Levels 840L–860L

Nonfiction Unit

Lexile Levels 820L–850L

Term 4

Fiction Unit

Lexile Levels 840L–870L

Nonfiction Unit

Lexile Levels 850L–870L

INTRODUCTION

Reading comprehension is the ability to understand and interpret text. To become confident and competent readers, students need to learn how to understand the literal meaning of a text and its vocabulary, and also its implied and inferred meaning.

This workbook is organised into four terms of work with 40 step-by-step lessons that focus on specific comprehension skills. To further support students, 8 grammar lessons target language usage. By looking carefully at words, clauses and sentences, students are better equipped to understand the texts they read. Each terms ends with a summative assessment that identifies students' strengths and rewards progress.

Step-by-step Comprehension

The 40 comprehension lessons teach key strategies for students to use when they read. Each lesson uses a levelled extract and focuses on a single comprehension strategy, with clear, easy-to-read instructions.

Students find key details in the text and highlight words and phrases. This ensures students have knowledge of the text before answering comprehension questions. The extracts are organised in a progressive sequence with clear modelling and built-in support. By focusing on a single strategy at a time, students develop their literal, inferential and critical comprehension skills, as well as extending their vocabulary.

Integrated Grammar

The eight grammar lessons in this book aim to help students understand how the English language system works, and how to apply this knowledge to texts.

Each lesson teaches a key concept in grammar. The focus is on connecting grammatical terms to text in meaningful ways. The instructional information box explains the concept and shows examples. Students then annotate a text and answer questions to identify the grammar in action. Questions increase in difficulty and include NAPLAN-style questions. The grammar lessons help students comprehend and connect with a broad range of texts.

The Reading Eggspress Online Lessons

Reading Eggspress provides a comprehensive and systematic online program that models, scaffolds and supports reading comprehension. The 220 lessons have been organised in a clear progression to develop reading comprehension skills for students in Years 1–6. Each lesson includes built-in motivational elements to reward efforts and boost students' enthusiasm for reading.

The workbook lessons can be completed as a stand-alone reading comprehension course, but when combined with the online lessons they act as a powerful boost to students' reading comprehension skills. Students using the online program show significant year-on-year improvements in both reading comprehension skills and higher reading levels, as highlighted in the program's detailed reporting module.

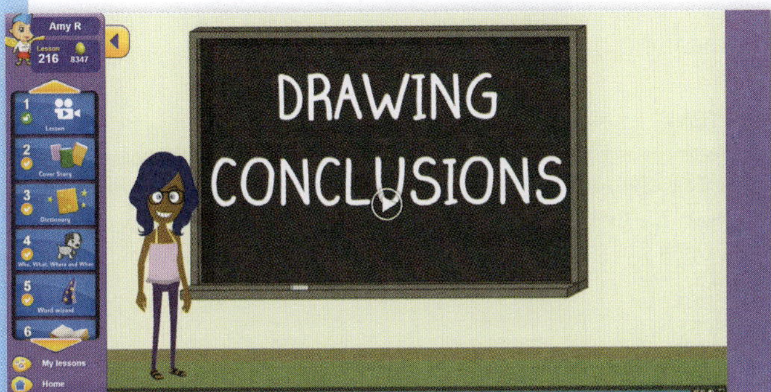

Engaging lessons

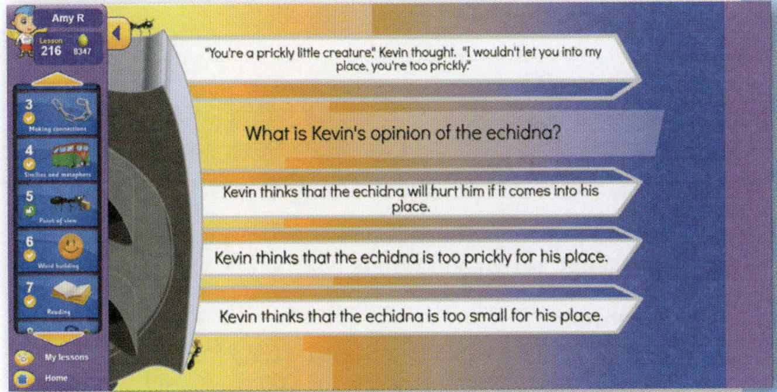

Interactive activities

The Library 4000+ ebooks

Students can practise their comprehension skills by reading ebooks in the Reading Eggspress Library. Search by topic, series, author, Lexile, reading age or book title to find the perfect book. With illustrated chapter books, full colour nonfiction books, poetry collections and a range of classics, there are texts to suit all readers and their capabilities.

New titles are added regularly with audio for all lower level books.

The Stadium

Compete in real time against students from around the country and around the world. These exciting head-to-head contests test skills in one of four areas—spelling, vocabulary, usage and grammar.

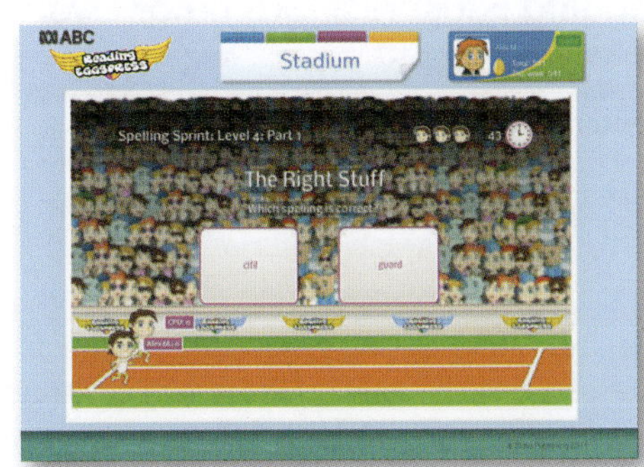

Reading Eggspress Workbooks and the Australian Curriculum

Each workbook lesson focuses on a core comprehension strategy or key concept in grammar. The texts, strategies and concepts were developed to align with the Australian Curriculum.

Year 4 Literacy

Interpreting, analysing and evaluating

ACELY1690 Identify characteristic features used in imaginative, informative and persuasive texts

ACELY1691 Read different types of texts

ACELY1692 Use comprehension strategies to build literal and inferred meaning

Year 4 Language

Text structure and organisation

ACELA1491 Understand how texts are made cohesive through the use of linking devices

ACELA1492 Recognise how quotation marks are used in texts to signal dialogue, titles and quoted (direct) speech

Text structure and organisation

ACELA1494 Investigate how quoted (direct) and reported (indirect) speech work in different types of text

ACELA1495 Understand how adverb groups/phrases and prepositional phrases work in different ways

Creating texts

Re-read and edit for meaning

Reading Eggspress Comprehension Strategy Overview

Comprehension	Strategy	Fiction Lessons	Nonfiction Lessons
Literal Looks for explicitly stated answers in the texts. Answers **Who**, **What**, **When** and **Where** questions.	Finding Facts and Information	105	128, 136
	Main Idea and Details	104	106, 117
	Sequencing Events	114	108
Inferential Finds implied information in the text. Looks for **text clues** and evidence that point to the correct answer.	Cause and Effect	112	129
	Compare and Contrast	135	107, 126, 139
	Drawing Conclusions		110, 140
	Making Inferences	124, 132	127
	Making Predictions	101	
	Figurative Language	102, 121	
	Important Information	125	120
Critical Asks for **connections** or **opinions** on information in the text. Uses text clues to support the connections.	Analysing Character Actions	115, 122	
	Making Connections	103, 131	137
	Visualisation	113, 134	119
	Point of View	111	109
	Audience and Purpose	123	118
	Fact or Opinion		138
Vocabulary Uses context clues and own knowledge to understand key words in the text	Word Study		116, 130

Reading Eggspress Grammar Overview

Grammar	Focus	Fiction Lessons	Nonfiction Lessons
Sentence Looks at how **clauses** are structured and how they come together to **build** cohesive sentences.	Pronouns	1	
	Determiners		4
	Quoted and Reported Speech	5	
	Fronted Adverbials		6
	Auxiliary Verbs	7	
Text Assesses paragraph **composition** to see how sentences work together to create cohesive texts.	Compound Sentences	3	
Punctuation Models correct punctuation **usage** for different types of words, clauses and sentences.	Capital Letters		2
	Plurals and Possessive Nouns		8

STUDENT RECORD SHEET

Use this page to record the number of questions you answered correctly for each lesson.

Term 1

Map 21 Fiction Lessons 780L–810L	**101** Making Predictions	**102** Figurative Language	**103** Making Connections	**104** Main Idea and Detail	**105** Finding Facts and Information	**Grammar 1** Pronouns	
Map 22 Nonfiction Lessons 790L–820L	**106** Main Idea and Details	**107** Compare and Contrast	**108** Sequencing Events	**109** Point of View	**110** Drawing Conclusions	**Grammar 2** Capital Letters	**Assessment 1** *One Minute Past Midnight*

Term 2

Map 23 Fiction Lessons 800L–840L	**111** Point of View	**112** Cause and Effect	**113** Visualisation	**114** Sequencing Events	**115** Analysing Character Behaviours	**Grammar 3** Compound Sentences	
Map 24 Nonfiction Lessons 810L–840L	**116** Word Study	**117** Main Idea and Details	**118** Audience and Purpose	**119** Visualisation	**120** Important Information	**Grammar 4** Determiners	**Assessment 2** *The Time Keepers*

Term 3

Map 25 Fiction Lessons 840L–860L	**121** Figurative Language	**122** Analysing Character Actions	**123** Audience and Purpose	**124** Making Inferences	**125** Important Information	**Grammar 5** Quoted and Reported Speech	
Map 26 Nonfiction Lessons 820L–850L	**126** Compare and Contrast	**127** Making Inferences	**128** Finding Facts and Information	**129** Cause and Effect	**130** Word Study	**Grammar 6** Fronted Adverbials	**Assessment 3** *The Crow*

Term 4

Map 27 Fiction Lessons 840L–870L	**131** Making Connections	**132** Making Inferences	**133** Word Study	**134** Visualisation	**135** Compare and Contrast	**Grammar 7** Auxiliary Verbs	
Map 28 Nonfiction Lessons 850L–870L	**136** Finding Facts and Information	**137** Making Connections	**138** Fact or Opinion?	**139** Compare and Contrast	**140** Drawing Conclusions	**Grammar 8** Plurals and Possessive Nouns	**Assessment 4** *What is Pollution?*

LESSON 101

The Goats

Making Predictions

We can predict what is going to happen in a text based on clues in the words and pictures and what we already know.

Read the passage.

Circle what the goats did to the children.

Underline why Mr Kent was pleased with the goats.

Put a box around where Mr Kent was when he saw the yabbies.

Highlight how Mr Kent was standing when he looked at the yabbies.

Colour why Mr Kent was excited.

Lots of children heard about the goats and came to visit. Morecambe and Wise put their heads down and butted them in all directions.

The children thought it was great fun—that is, the ones that got away did. The children who didn't escape went home crying and told their mothers.

Mr Kent smiled when he saw what was happening. "These goats are as good as a watchdog," he said. "This'll put a stop to whoever is nicking our strawberries."

Mr Kent wasn't so happy the next day.

He was at the dam. He leaned forward, then called excitedly to Mrs Kent, "We've got some baby yabbies! Hurray!"

Circle the correct answers.

1. What three predictions can you make about what will happen next in the story?
   - a One of the goats will butt Mr Kent.
   - b Mr Kent will push the goats into the dam.
   - c Mr Kent will be angry.
   - d Mrs Kent will push Mr Kent into the dam.
   - e Mr Kent will get wet.
   - f The goats will eat the baby yabbies

2. What **evidence** is there in the text to support your predictions? Select two answers.
   - a Mr Kent was excited about the yabbies.
   - b Some of the children got away from the goats.
   - c The goats have shown that they like to butt people.
   - d Someone had been stealing the Kents' strawberries.
   - e The children didn't like it when the goats butted them.
   - f Mr Kent was in the right position to get butted.

AC9E4LY05 Use comprehension strategies such as predicting to build inferred meaning

Read the passage.

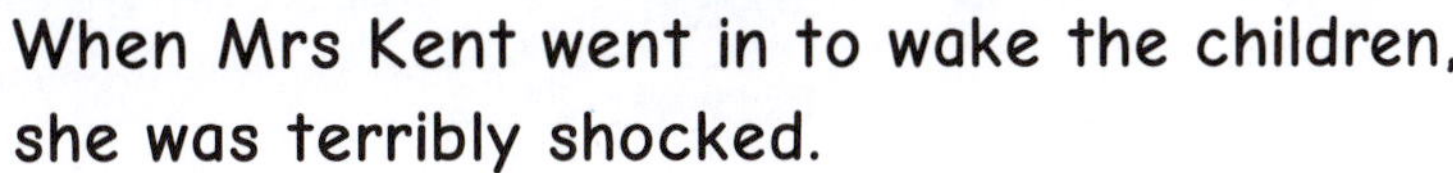

(Circle) how Mrs Kent felt when she saw that the children were missing.

Put a [box] around what Wise did to Mrs Kent.

When Mrs Kent went in to wake the children, she was terribly shocked.

"The children aren't here!" she cried to Mr Kent. "Where could they be?"

Mr and Mrs Kent looked everywhere. They looked inside the house and outside the house.

Morecambe started butting his head against Mr Kent as he searched near the shed.

Wise started pushing against Mrs Kent while she peered under the car.

"The goats are trying to tell us something," said Mr Kent.

"Let's untie them and see what they do," replied Mrs Kent.

Highlight what Morecambe did to Mr Kent.

Underline what Mr Kent said to Mrs Kent.

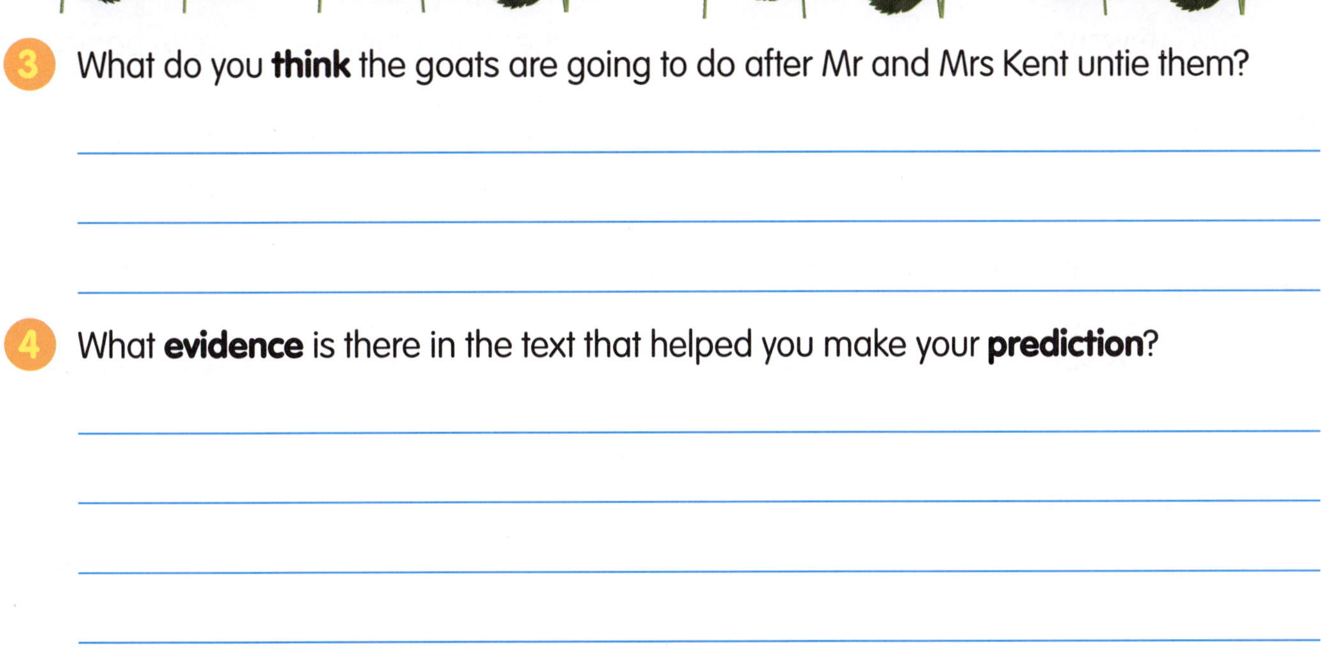

3 What do you **think** the goats are going to do after Mr and Mrs Kent untie them?

4 What **evidence** is there in the text that helped you make your **prediction**?

AC9E4LY05 Use comprehension strategies such as predicting to build inferred meaning

LESSON 102

Getting Rid of Wrinkles

Figurative Language

Similes and metaphors are examples of figurative language. They use comparisons to help us visualise pictures. Similes compare one thing to something else using the words *like* or *as*. Metaphors make a more direct comparison. They do not use *like* or *as*.

Read the passage.

Underline the simile in paragraph 1.

Circle the animal that Great Grandpop compares Great Grandma to.

Tessa's Great Grandma Em had a face like a sheet of scrunched up newspaper. Great Grandpop Alfred teased her lots.

"You look like a hippopotamus that has been bathing in the river too long," he said at breakfast.

"The bags under your eyes could carry the treasure from a sunken pirate ship," he said at lunch.

Colour the simile in paragraph 2.

Highlight the metaphor in paragraph 3.

Circle the correct answers.

1. What is Great Grandma Em's face **compared** to?
   - a a sheet
   - b a hippopotamus
   - c a newspaper
   - d a sheet of scrunched up newspaper
2. The figure of speech in paragraph 1 is a **simile**. Which word tells us this?
   - a a
   - b like
   - c of
   - d sheet
3. What does the **simile** in paragraph 1 **suggest** about Great Grandma Em's face? Her face is …
   - a very thin.
   - b quite hard.
   - c full of wrinkles.
   - d very smooth.
4. What does Great Grandpop Alfred **compare** the bags under Great Grandma's eyes to? Bags that can carry …
   - a pirate treasure.
   - b pirates.
   - c ships.
   - d sunken ships.
5. The figure of speech in paragraph 3 is a **metaphor**. What does it **suggest** about the bags under Great Grandma's eyes? The bags under her eyes are …
   - a colourful.
   - b valuable.
   - c large.
   - d sparkly.

AC9E4LE04 Examine the use of literary devices and deliberate word play in literary texts to shape meaning

Read the passage.

Underline three similes in paragraph 1.

Circle the words in paragraph 1 that show that the figures of speech are similes.

By the time the big day arrived, Great Gran's skin was as smooth as whipped cream, her cheeks were as rosy as ripe strawberries, and her eyes were like rich, dark chocolate drops.

"You're as lovely as the day I first saw you running across the paddock from the Maloney's prize bull," said Great Grandpop as he waltzed her around the living room.

Put a box around two adjectives that describe Great Gran's eyes.

Highlight the adjective that suggests that Great Gran had no wrinkles.

6 Great Gran's skin is compared to whipped cream. What picture of her skin does this create?

7 Great Gran's cheeks are described as being rosy. They are compared to ripe strawberries. Do you think this is a good comparison? Why, or why not?

8 What picture do we get of Great Gran's eyes from the comparison: *Her eyes were like rich, dark chocolate drops?*

9 Choose one of the **similes** in paragraph 1 and write it as a **metaphor**.

LESSON 103

Tokyo Techno

Making Connections

Linking a text to other texts you have read is a great way to build understanding. Look for key words and phrases in the texts to make the connections.

Read the passages.

Anita unfolded a map of Japan.

"It says the capital of Japan is Tokyo. That's where we're going." She read on, "Japan is made up of four main islands and over 3000 little ones." Anita marked Tokyo, on the island of Honshu, with a red spot.

In the corner of the map Jason pointed to a white flag with a red circle in the middle. "That's the Japanese flag," he said. "The word Japan actually means *source of the sun*."

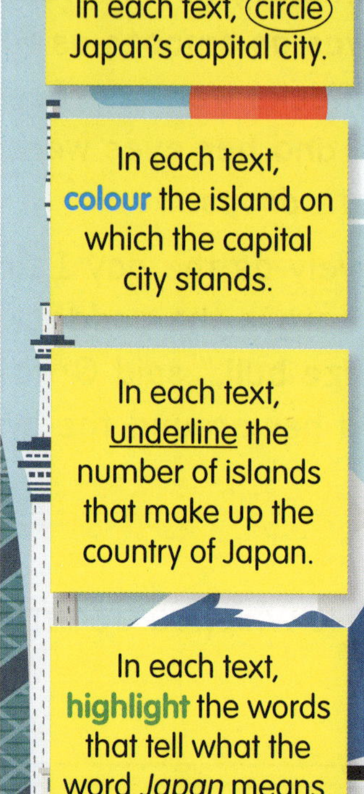

In each text, circle Japan's capital city.

In each text, colour the island on which the capital city stands.

In each text, underline the number of islands that make up the country of Japan.

In each text, highlight the words that tell what the word *Japan* means.

Japan is a country in the Pacific Ocean. It consists of four main islands and thousands of smaller ones. The capital city, Tokyo, is on the island of Honshu.

Japan is known as the *Land of the Rising Sun*. This is because its name means *sun origin*.

Japan is on the Pacific Ring of Fire. It experiences over 1500 earthquakes every year. In 2011, a huge earthquake and tsunami caused a lot of damage.

Circle the correct answers.

1. Which information appears in both texts?
   - a Japan consists of many islands.
   - b The capital city of Japan is Tokyo.
   - c Japan is on the Pacific Ring of Fire.
   - d Tokyo is on the island of Honshu.
   - e Japan often experiences earthquakes.
   - f Four of Japan's islands are bigger than the others.
   - g Japan is known as the *Land of the Rising Sun*.
   - h The word Japan means *where the sun comes from*.

AC9E4LY05 Use comprehension strategies such as connecting to evaluate texts

Read the passages.

Jason looked out the train window. Beyond the rice fields he could see a huge snow-capped mountain. "That mountain looks like an old volcano."

"It is. Japan is full of volcanoes," said Toshi. "That's Mount Fuji, Japan's most famous mountain."

Jason pulled an instant camera out of their bag and took a photo. On the bottom he wrote 'Mount Fuji, JAPAN—famous old volcano.'

Underline the words in each text that give the same information about Mount Fuji.

Colour the words in each text that give different information about Mount Fuji.

In each text, highlight the phrases that tell what passengers on the train often do when they pass Mount Fuji.

Mount Fuji is Japan's highest and most famous mountain. It has been worshipped as a sacred mountain for centuries.

Mount Fuji is an active volcano. It last erupted in 1708.

A good way to view Mount Fuji is from the train on the trip between Tokyo and Osaka. Tourists can often be seen taking photographs of Mount Fuji from the train windows.

2 What do both texts tell us about Mount Fuji?

3 What extra information about Mount Fuji do we get if we look at the texts separately?

4 Imagine you are planning a trip to Japan. How would these two texts help you decide on the best way to view Mount Fuji?

LESSON 104

Tiddalik the Frog

Finding the Main Idea and Supporting Details

To discover what a text is about, you need to look for the main idea or key point. Facts and details in the text can help you find the main idea.

Read the passage.

Circle the word that tells how Tiddalik was feeling.

Highlight the noun that tells what Tiddalik needed.

Put a box around the action verb that tells what Tiddalik did.

Underline the sentence that contains the main idea.

Narrator: Long ago in the Dreaming, Tiddalik the frog woke very thirsty one morning.

Tiddalik: I need water, I need water, I need water ...

Narrator: So Tiddalik drank all the water he could find.

Tiddalik: *[gulp] [gulp] [gulp] [gulp]*

Narrator: He drank so much that every billabong and creek and every river and stream was emptied.

Circle the correct answers.

1. What is the **main idea** or **key point** of the text?
   - a Tiddalik the frog was very thirsty.
   - b Tiddalik the frog gulped down the water.
   - c Tiddalik the frog lived long ago.
   - d Tiddalik the frog drank all the water.

2. Which word best **supports** the **main idea**?
   - a water
   - b emptied
   - c drank
   - d thirsty

3. Which phrase best **supports** the **main idea**?
   - a every billabong and creek and every river and every stream
   - b need water
   - c Long ago in the Dreaming
   - d woke very thirsty

AC9E4LY05 Use comprehension strategies to build literal meaning

Read the passage.

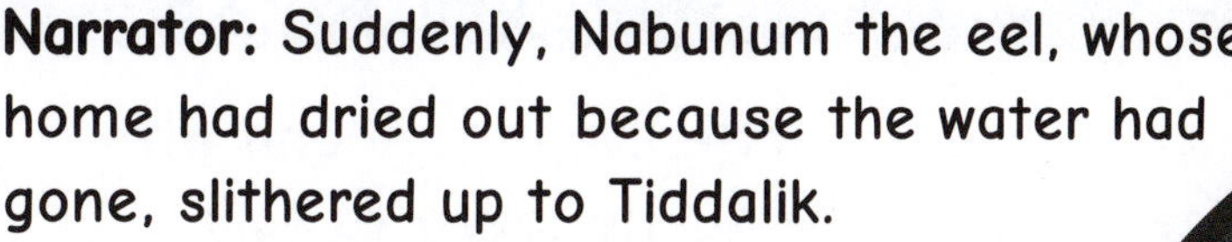

Underline the name of the animal that tried to make Tiddalik laugh.

Highlight the reason Tiddalik started giggling.

Narrator: Suddenly, Nabunum the eel, whose home had dried out because the water had gone, slithered up to Tiddalik.

Nabunum: Time for you to laugh, froggy.

Narrator: Nabunum began to dance, slowly at first, then faster and faster, wriggling into all sorts of shapes, knots and twists. It worked! Tiddalik started giggling.

Kookaburra: I think he's going to burst.

Wombat: Stand back, here comes the water!

Colour what Kookaburra thought was going to happen.

Put a box around the reason Wombat told everyone to stand back.

4 What is the **main idea** or **key point** of the text?

____

____

____

5 List three **details** that **support** the **main idea**.

a ______________________________

____

____

b ______________________________

____

____

c ______________________________

____

____

LESSON 105

The Turtle Who Couldn't Stop Talking

Finding Facts and Information

To find facts and information in a text, we usually ask the questions **Who? What? Where?** or **When?** The answers can be clearly seen in the text.

Read the passage.

Circle who lived in the pond.

Underline when the pond dried up.

Put a box around when the events in the story happened.

Highlight the turtle's words.

Long ago, a turtle lived in a pond with two swans. The turtle loved to talk. After a long drought, the pond dried up. The two swans realised they would have to find another pond.

"Don't leave me!" begged the turtle.

"But you can't fly," said the swans. "How can you come with us?" The turtle pleaded and pleaded. The swans at last came up with an idea.

Circle the correct answers.

1. **How many** creatures lived in the pond?
   - a one
   - b three
   - c two
   - d four

2. **When** did the pond dry up?
   - a long after the drought
   - b during the drought
   - c after the long drought
   - d in the middle of the drought

3. **Who** decided to find another pond?
   - a the turtle
   - b one of the swans
   - c the fish
   - d both swans

4. **What** did the turtle say?
   - a "I can't fly!"
   - b "Come with me!"
   - c "Don't leave me!"
   - d "Please help me!"

5. **When** did the events in the story happen?
   - a not so long ago
   - b a long time ago
   - c during the drought
   - d one hundred years ago

AC9E4LY05 Use comprehension strategies to build literal meaning

Read the passage.

Underline what the turtle wanted to say when they flew high.

Highlight what the townspeople shouted.

When they flew high, the turtle wanted to say "Look at the beautiful view!", but he remembered the swans' warning not to say a word.

They passed over a small town. People looked up and shouted, "Look at that silly turtle!"

The turtle wanted to cry out, "Mind your own business," but he again remembered the warning. As they flew on, more villagers spotted them. People began pointing and crying, "Crazy swans! Crazy turtle!"

The turtle couldn't stand it any longer. He yelled out, "Go away foolish people!" But he let go of the stick in his mouth and fell to the ground, landing on his back and cracking his shell into a thousand pieces.

Put a box around the reason the turtle opened his mouth.

Colour what happened when the turtle let go of the stick.

6 **What** did the turtle want to say when he looked down at the view?

7 **Where** were they flying when the people shouted, "Look at that silly turtle"?

8 **When** did the turtle open his mouth?

9 **What** happened when the turtle opened his mouth?

Pronouns

Pronouns are used in place of nouns.

- **Personal pronouns** are used in place of the people or things we are talking about. For example: **Joe is talking. He is talking.**
- **Possessive pronouns** show ownership. For example: **That is Joe's cap. That is his cap.**

Read the extract.

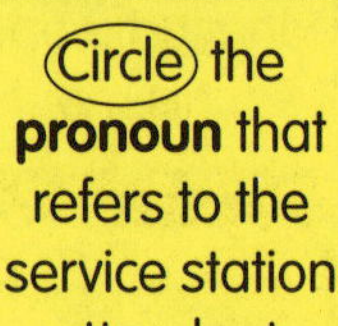

Circle the **pronoun** that refers to the service station attendant.

Colour the **pronoun** that refers to the narrator.

Put a box around the **pronoun** that takes the place of *the car's*.

Highlight the **pronoun** that shows that the breath belongs to Max.

Camp Blizzard

Dad asks the service station attendant a quick question and she points in the direction we've just come. Dad hops back into the car with snacks clutched in his hands.

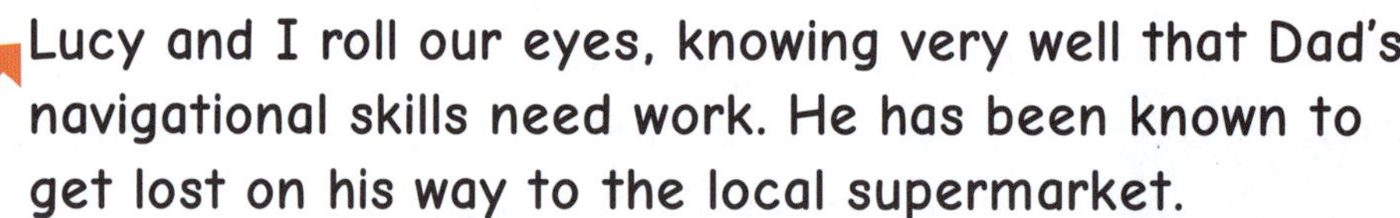

Lucy and I roll our eyes, knowing very well that Dad's navigational skills need work. He has been known to get lost on his way to the local supermarket.

I cheer when I see the Mount Falls National Park sign. Mum stops chewing her fingernails.

"Shouldn't be long now," sighs Dad, as the car rattles and bumps its way over the corrugated road.

The campsite finally comes into view. "There it is!" shouts Dad. "What do you think, Max?"

I'm not sure what to say. My breath is turning to vapour and the chill is starting to creep into my bones.

Circle the correct answers.

1 In the first paragraph, who does the **pronoun** *his* refer to?

a the narrator b Dad c the service station attendant d Lucy

2 Which **pronoun** shows that the eyes belong to Lucy and the narrator?

a we b us c our d their

3 In paragraph 3, who does the **pronoun** *her* refer to?

a Mum b the service station attendant c Lucy d Dad

4 In paragraph 5, which **pronoun** stands in place of *campsite*?

a he b our c she d it

5 In the final paragraph, which **pronoun** shows that the bones belong to Max?

a I b me c my d his

AC9E4LA04 Identify how text connectives are used to sequence and connect ideas

6 **Circle the pronoun that correctly completes each sentence.**

a	Mum left _______ bag in the caravan.	she	hers	her
b	_______ toasted marshmallows over the campfire.	Us	We	Our
c	The man showed _______ where the campsite was.	their	they	them
d	We loaded _______ equipment into the camper van.	us	our	ours
e	We could hear _______ footsteps approaching the tent.	it	it's	its

7 **Fill each gap with a pronoun from the list.**

my	our	mine	him	you	their	yours

This sleeping bag is **A** ________________ and that one is **B** ________________.

8 **Which sentence is correct? Tick.**

a ☐ Max and me went camping.

b ☐ Me and Max went camping.

c ☐ Max and I went camping.

d ☐ I and Max went camping.

9 **Replace the underlined nouns with pronouns.**

Dad gave Sam a fishing rod for Sam's **a** ____________ birthday. Sam said the fishing rod **b** ____________ was the best present Sam **c** ____________ had ever had. Sam **d** ____________ said Sam **e** ____________ was looking forward to using the fishing rod **f** ____________ the next time Sam and his dad **g** ____________ went camping.

LESSON 106

Homes

Finding the Main Idea and Supporting Details

To discover what a text is about, you need to look for the main idea or key point. Facts and details in the text can help you find the main idea.

Read the passage.

Circle when most homes received electricity.

Underline the sentence that sums up the main idea of the passage.

Highlight what electric light bulbs replaced.

Most homes received electricity during the early 1900's. Rural homes had to wait longer. Many homes in developing countries still do not have electricity.

Electricity changed the way homes worked. Electric ovens and heaters replaced gas and wood-burning stoves. Electric light bulbs replaced kerosene lamps and gas lights. Electric refrigerators replaced iceboxes. Electricity also led to the invention of the telephone.

Colour what electric ovens and heaters replaced.

Put a box around what refrigerators replaced.

Circle the invention that allows us to communicate with people who are far away.

Circle the correct answers.

1. What is the passage **mainly** about?
   - a the reasons some homes do not have electricity
   - b the reason the telephone was invented
   - c when most homes received electricity
   - d how electricity has changed the way homes work

2. Which three **details support the main idea**?
   - a Electric ovens and heaters replaced gas and wood-burning stoves.
   - b City homes received electricity before rural homes.
   - c Many homes in developing countries still do not have electricity.
   - d Electric refrigerators replaced iceboxes.
   - e Most homes received electricity over a hundred years ago.
   - f Electric light bulbs replaced kerosene lamps and gas lights.

AC9E4LY05 Use comprehension strategies to build literal meaning

Read the passage.

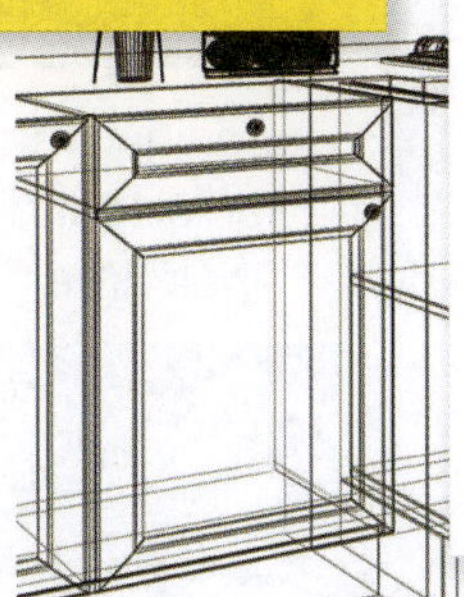

<u>Underline</u> the sentence that sums up the main idea of the passage.

Highlight how bathrooms have changed through the years.

The layout of rooms in a home has changed as society has changed.

As plumbing improved, bathrooms became rooms inside the home, rather than outside.

Kitchens only became the centre of homes in the last 60 years. Filled with new appliances, they are no longer hidden rooms used for hard, dirty work. They are linked to open-plan living and dining areas.

Informal living areas at the rear of homes replaced formal living rooms at the front. Living areas were linked to terraces and gardens to create outdoor rooms.

Colour how kitchens have changed in the last 60 years.

Put a box around where informal living areas are found in modern homes.

3 Which sentence sums up what the passage is about?

4 List three **details** that **support** the **main idea**.

a

b

c

LESSON 107

Sea Life

Compare and Contrast

When we compare and contrast information, we look for the similarities and differences between details in the text.

Read the passage.

Circle what kind of animal whales and seals are.

Highlight the reason whales and seals cannot breathe under water.

Colour what whales and seals feed their babies.

Underline where baby whales are born.

Put a box around where seal pups are born.

Underline where seals spend their time.

Whales, dolphins, seals and sea lions are marine mammals.

Mammals cannot breathe under water because they have lungs, not gills. They must come to the surface to breathe.

The babies of whales and dolphins are born under water. The mothers push the babies to the surface to take their first breath.

Seals and sea lions spend most of their time in the water, feeding on fish, squid and penguins. They also spend time on land, resting. Seal pups are born on land and like all marine mammal babies, they are fed on milk.

Circle the correct answers.

1. In which three ways are whales and seals **similar**?
   - a Both give birth to their babies on land.
   - b Both spend time resting on land.
   - c Both must come to the surface to breathe.
   - d Both are mammals.
   - e Both spend all of their time in the water.
   - f Both feed their babies milk.

2. In which two ways are seals **different** from whales?
   - a Their babies are born on land.
   - b They have lungs, not gills.
   - c They are marine mammals.
   - d They spend time in the water and on land.
   - e They spend all their time in the water.

AC9E4LY05 Use comprehension strategies to expand topic knowledge and ideas, and evaluate texts

Read the passage.

Circle what wading birds and albatrosses eat.

Underline where oystercatchers live and feed.

Colour how albatrosses catch their food.

Many birds depend on the sea for their food. Wading birds, penguins, albatrosses, gulls and pelicans hunt and eat fish and other sea creatures.

Wading birds, such as oystercatchers, live and feed along the shore. Long, spindly legs help them wade through shallow water. Their thin beaks dig around for small animals in the water and mud.

Out over the deeper ocean, birds need to be able to fly for long periods of time. The albatross has very long wings so that it can glide for hours. It can stay in the air for weeks at a time. These seabirds dive into the water to catch their food.

Penguins cannot fly at all. They use their flippers and their webbed feet to swim very fast and catch fish.

Highlight how oystercatchers find their food.

Put a box around where albatrosses find their food.

Colour how penguins are different from other seabirds.

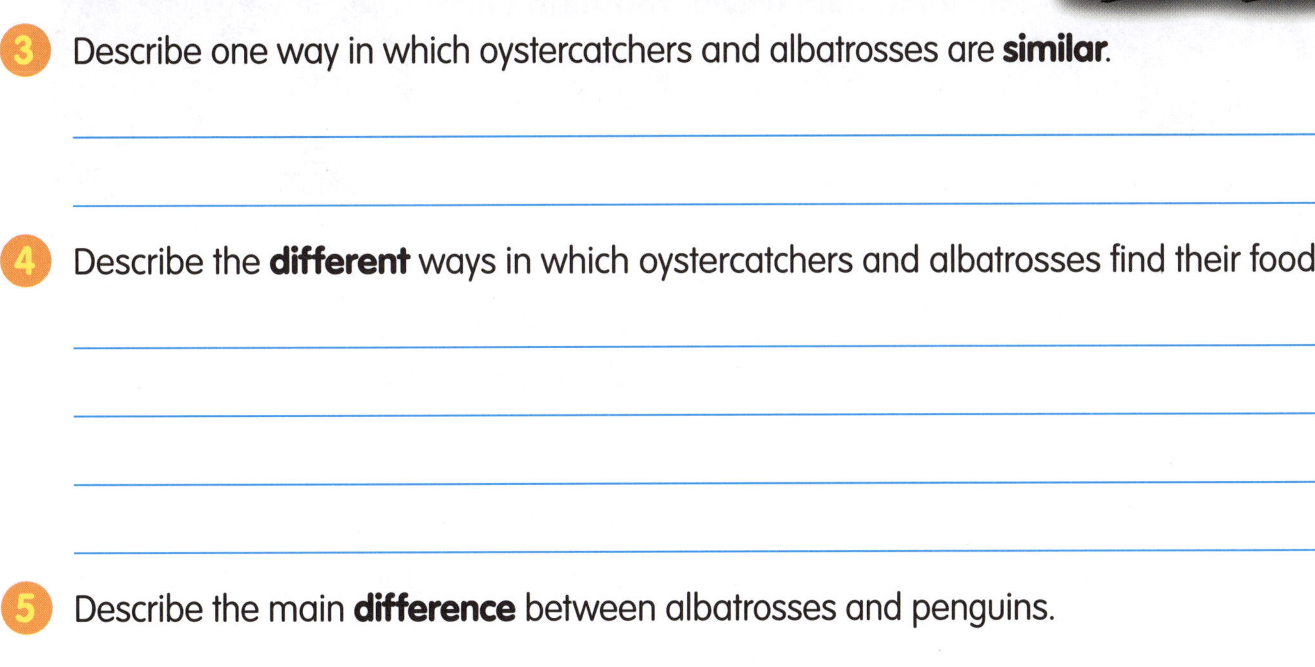

3 Describe one way in which oystercatchers and albatrosses are **similar**.

4 Describe the **different** ways in which oystercatchers and albatrosses find their food.

5 Describe the main **difference** between albatrosses and penguins.

LESSON 108

Polar Animals

Sequencing Events

To identify the sequence of events in a text, look at numbers and words that give clues to the order in which things happen.

Read the passage.

Circle what happens just before the female goes to feed.

Highlight how long the female stays at sea.

Put a box around when the egg hatches.

Emperor penguins are the only warm-blooded animals that spend winter in Antarctica.

In May, the female lays a single egg, and then walks to the sea to feed. She stays at sea until the egg hatches.

The male stays behind to look after the egg. He balances the egg on his feet and protects it under a thick roll of skin called a brood pouch. During this time, the male does not eat.

The egg hatches after about two months. The chick stays in the brood pouch until it can survive on its own.

The female returns to feed the chick. The male then leaves to find food.

Underline how the male protects the egg.

Colour how long the chick stays in the brood pouch.

Circle the correct answers.

1 **When** does the female Emperor penguin go to the sea to feed?

a after the egg hatches
b while the egg is hatching
c after she lays the egg
d before she lays the egg

2 **What happens while** the female is feeding?

a The male looks after the egg.
b The other penguins look after the egg.
c The male goes in search of food.
d The male grows a brood pouch.

3 **When** does the female return from the sea?

a just before the egg hatches
b once the egg hatches
c while the egg is hatching
d once the chick can survive on its own

AC9E4LY05 Use comprehension strategies to build literal and inferred meaning

Read the passage.

Circle when caribou migrate north.

Put a box around the season that comes after spring.

Highlight what caribou do in summer.

Caribou are wild reindeer. They live in the Arctic regions of Russia, Alaska, Canada and Greenland.

Caribou live in herds. The herd protects calves from predators such as bears, lynxes and golden eagles.

In spring, caribou migrate about 5000 kilometres north to breed on the Arctic tundra. All summer, they eat leaves and grass to build up their fat stores for winter.

When the tundra becomes cold and windy, the herds migrate south to the forests. They spend winter in forests, feeding on plants such as lichens and mosses.

Colour when caribou migrate south.

Underline the season that comes before spring.

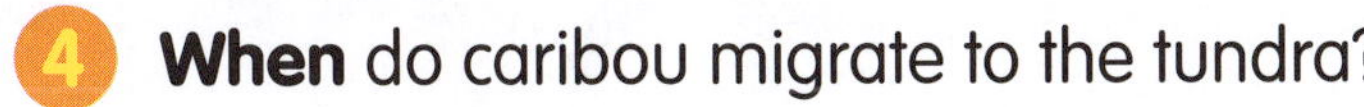

4 **When** do caribou migrate to the tundra?

____

5 Use the information in the text to help you complete the following sentences.

During **a** _____________, caribou build up their fat stores for **b** _____________.

The herds migrate south when **c** ____

____.

During **d** _____________, caribou live in forests, where they feed on plants such as lichens and mosses.

When spring returns, **e** ____

____

____.

LESSON 109

Letter to the Editor

Point of View

To identify a point of view, we have to look at the way authors express their opinions and views (what they think and believe) about a subject.

Read the passage.

Underline three words that show what the writer thinks of Mr Frame's remark.

Highlight two words that show the writer's opinion on the number of overweight children.

Put a box around how the writer thinks children should get to school.

Dear Sir/Madam,

Mr Frame's remark ("That's What Cars Are For", *Tagownda Times*, 12.10.2010) about the role of cars in our community completely misses the point. The debate is about cars picking up and dropping off children outside Tagownda Primary School; it is not an attack on the motor car. The simple question remains: why are so many children arriving at school by car?

The National Children's Nutrition and Activity Survey recently revealed that almost one quarter of children aged two to 16 are overweight. This is a shocking statistic. Encouraging children to walk to school might help to address this major health issue.

Circle the correct answers.

1. What is the writer's **opinion** of Mr Frame's remark about the role of cars in the community? He thinks Mr Frame …
   - a is silly.
   - b knows what he is talking about.
   - c has a good point.
   - d is missing the point.
2. How does the writer **feel** about the number of children who are overweight?
   - a surprised
   - b shocked
   - c confused
   - d disappointed
3. How serious does the writer **believe** the problem of overweight children is? He believes it is …
   - a a major health issue.
   - b a minor problem.
   - c quite serious.
   - d nothing to worry about.
4. From the writer's **point of view**, how should most children be getting to school?
   - a by car
   - b by bus
   - c on a bike
   - d on foot

AC9E4LY05 Use comprehension strategies to build literal and inferred meaning

Read the passage.

Highlight the evidence the writer gives to support his view that using cars less will make the streets safer.

Underline the writer's offer to get more children walking to school.

Colour the pronoun that shows that the letter is written from Ted Chu's point of view.

Using cars less often reduces our impact on the environment. Safety is another concern: the more we all walk, the safer our streets become. Tagownda Police Station reports that three accidents involving pedestrians have occurred within half a kilometre of the front gate of Tagownda Primary School within the last 18 months alone.

As convener of our local "Get Out and About" walking group, I am ready and willing to work with the staff, students and families of Tagownda Primary School to increase the number of students walking to school. In the meantime, we should all be asking ourselves: if it's not hailing, snowing or pouring with rain, how about walking for a change?

Ted Chu

5 How does the writer support his **view** that using cars less will make our streets safer?

____

____

6 What other benefit does the writer **believe** using cars less will have?

____

____

7 Explain the writer's offer of help to get more students walking to school.

____

____

8 How do we know that the letter is written from Ted Chu's **point of view**?

____

____

LESSON 110

Materials

Drawing Conclusions

To draw conclusions from a text, we have to use clues to make our own judgements. The clues help us find the answers that are hiding in the text.

Read the passage.

Circle where sand, limestone and soda ash are melted.

Put a box around the word that shows that glass can be used over and over.

Underline what happens to molten glass.

Glass is made by mixing sand, limestone and soda ash in a furnace. The molten glass is poured into a mould or laid out in sheets. It hardens as it cools.

Glass breaks easily. This property can be changed by adding chemicals or by changing the way glass cools. If you reheat glass, then quickly cool it, the glass becomes much stronger.

Pyrex glass is a special type of glass. It does not expand when it is heated as much as normal glass.

Glass can be recycled over and over again.

Circle the correct answers.

1. Which is the best **conclusion**? Glass is made by melting a mixture of minerals at …
   - a low temperatures.
   - b freezing temperatures.
   - c very high temperatures.

2. Which is the best **clue** to question 1's answer.
   - a poured
   - b furnace
   - c mould
   - d sheets

3. Which is the best **conclusion**? Glass can be made into …
   - a one shape only.
   - b flat shapes only.
   - c long shapes only.
   - d lots of different shapes.

4. Which two words are the best **clues** to question 3's answer?
   - a *mould* and *sheets*
   - b *sand* and *limestone*
   - c *hardens* and *cools*
   - d *mixing* and *poured*

5. Which is the best **conclusion**? Glass …
   - a is an eco-friendly material.
   - b is harmful to the environment.
   - c has very few uses.
   - d is a very soft material.

AC9E4LY05 Use comprehension strategies to build inferred meaning

Read the passage.

Circle the different ways of collecting metals from ores.

Highlight what makes iron and steel corrode faster.

Underline how iron ore is changed into steel.

Put a box around what is added to steel to make stainless steel.

Most metals come from minerals. Rocks that contain minerals are called ores. They are crushed or heated to collect the metal.

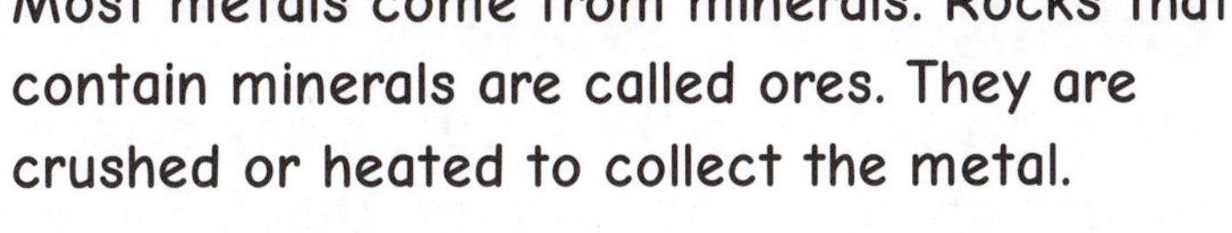

Iron comes from iron ore. It is made into steel by adding carbon.

Metals can corrode. When rust eats away at iron or steel, it corrodes. Rust is a flaky, brown substance that forms when oxygen, water and iron combine. This process is faster if the water is salty.

An alloy is a mixture of metals. For example, stainless steel is an alloy of steel and chromium. Alloys have different properties. They can be stronger, lighter and softer than other metals.

6. The text **suggests** that there are different ways of collecting metals from ores. Which words are the **clues**?

7. Why can we **conclude** that iron and steel will corrode faster in sea water?

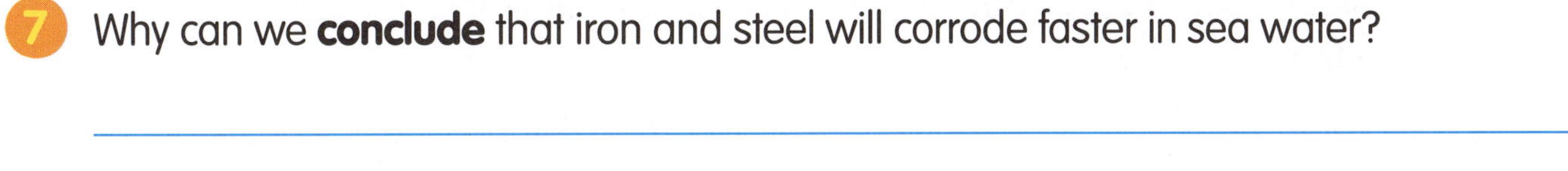

8. Why can we **conclude** that steel and stainless steel have different properties?

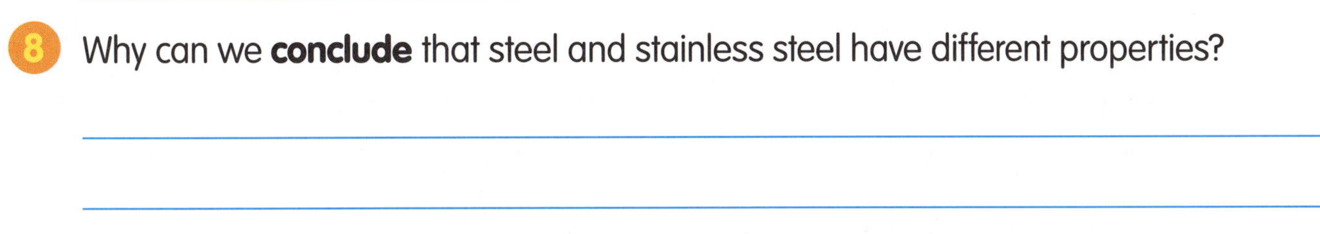

GRAMMAR LESSON 2

Capital Letters

The following words always start with a capital letter:
- the first word in a **sentence.**
- the personal pronoun *I*.
- proper nouns (the names of **specific people, places, animals or things**).
- titles when they form part of a person's name. For example: **Mrs Jones, Doctor Wilson.**
- adjectives that are formed from proper nouns. For example: **an Australian story, Japanese cars.**

Read the extract.

In this sentence, circle the **proper noun**.

In this sentence, colour the **name** of the **person** who led the voyage.

In this paragraph, put a box around three **proper nouns**.

In this paragraph, highlight the **name** given to the first eleven ships to transport convicts to Australia.

Colonising the World

From the 1400s to the 1700s, many explorers set out from Europe on great sea voyages. These European explorers came from countries like France, Portugal, Spain and Great Britain.

One voyage was led by Lieutenant James Cook. In 1770 he sailed into a bay on the east coast of what would one day be called Australia. He named it Botany Bay and claimed the entire coast for Great Britain.

At the time, there were few jobs in Great Britain. Many people turned to crime just to survive. To ease the pressure on overcrowded jails, Great Britain transported criminals to its colonies in America, and later Australia.

In 1787, Governor Arthur Philip left Great Britain for New South Wales with eleven ships. On board were about 1350 people, including 751 convicts. These ships are known as the First Fleet.

Circle the correct answers.

1. Why does the word **European** start with a capital letter? It is an adjective formed from …

   a a proper noun. b a verb. c a common noun. d an abstract noun.

2. Why does the word **Lieutenant** start with a capital letter? It is someone's …

   a first name. b title. c surname. d middle name.

3. In paragraph 3, why does the word **Many** start with a capital letter? It is …

   a a personal pronoun. b the name of a specific thing.
   c the first word in the sentence. d an adjective formed from a proper noun.

4. Why does the word **New** in **New South Wales** start with a capital letter? It is …

   a the first word in a sentence. b part of a proper noun.
   c part of a person's title. d an adjective formed from a proper noun.

AC9E4LY06 Edit written texts for simple punctuation

5 In each sentence, one word has been written incorrectly. Circle it, and write the correction in the space.

a The Indian ocean lies to the west of Australia. ______

b In 1770 lieutenant James Cook reached Botany Bay. ______

c Lieutenant James Cook's ship was the HMS endeavour. ______

d The first governor of New South Wales was Arthur phillip. ______

6 Which sentence has the correct capital letters? Tick.

a ☐ the first convicts arrived in Australia in January 1788.

b ☐ The First Convicts arrived in Australia in January 1788.

c ☐ The first convicts arrived in Australia in January 1788.

d ☐ The first convicts arrived in Australia in january 1788.

7 Circle the word that correctly completes each sentence.

a	There were many ______ people on the boat.	Britain	British
b	Some ______ explorers went to North America.	France	French
c	Vasco da Gama was a famous ______ explorer.	Portuguese	Portugal
d	At first, Great Britain sent convicts to its ______ colonies.	America	American

8 In each sentence, use a red pen to fill in the capital letters.

a the convicts' names were mary adams and charles allen.

b governor arthur phillip raised the british flag at sydney cove.

c the bass strait separates tasmania from the australian mainland.

d the aboriginal people have lived in australia for thousands of years.

ASSESSMENT 1:

One Minute Past Midnight

Lexile: 740

Samuel awoke with a start. Except for a thin sliver of light that shone through a crack in the curtains, his room was dark and still. The luminous hands of his bedside clock read one minute past midnight. What was it that had woken him? Samuel sat up in bed, his body tense, and listened intently. At first there was nothing but the sound of his ragged breathing. Then he heard it — a faint clicking sound, neither loud nor soft. Very quietly, Samuel got out of bed and crept out to the hallway, eerily lit by a waning moon. He paused, head tilted to one side. He could just hear the sound — click, click, click — above the loud thumping of his heart. It seemed to be coming from the study at the end of the hall. Samuel stole cautiously towards the closed door. With trembling fingers, he took hold of the knob and turned it slowly. Gently he nudged the door open.

A patch of moonlight lit up the faded carpet on the floor. Samuel peered into the gloom. The sound was coming from a dark corner of the room. He fumbled for the light switch and snapped it on. Light flooded the room and a wave of relief swept over Samuel when he saw what was causing the clicking sound. His father must have forgotten to switch off the fan. One of the blades was bent and each time it spun around, it hit the guard, making a clicking noise. The tension drained from Samuel's body as he strode across the room and switched off the fan. Satisfied that he had taken care of the problem, he turned off the light and left the study.

Samuel stepped back into the hall and headed towards his room. Suddenly he stopped. The hairs on the back of his neck rose. There was that noise again. Click, click, click. But this time, it was coming from his room!

Circle the correct answers.

1 What woke Samuel? **LITERAL**

- **a** light coming through the curtains
- **b** his noisy breathing
- **c** a clicking sound
- **d** his alarm clock

2 Why was Samuel able to see the time on his bedside clock? **INFERENTIAL**

a The moon cast a light on the clock.
b He used a flashlight.
c The hands of the clock glowed in the dark.
d He switched on the light.

3 How did Samuel feel as he walked towards the study? **INFERENTIAL**

a excited
b curious
c annoyed
d scared

4 In this text, what does the word 'stole' mean? **VOCABULARY**

a moved quietly
b robbed
c snatched
d stumbled

5 Which group of words tells you that Samuel was nervous about entering the study? **INFERENTIAL**

a took hold of
b turned it slowly
c with trembling fingers
d nudged the door open

6 What was the cause of the clicking noise? **LITERAL**

a the light switch
b the floorboards
c the fan
d the clock

7 What does the word 'strode' suggest about the way Samuel walked? **INFERENTIAL**
It suggests that Samuel walked …

a slowly.
b confidently.
c hesitantly.
d on tiptoes.

8 What type of story is this? **CRITICAL**

a adventure
b humorous
c mystery
d factual

9 What is the main purpose of this text? **CRITICAL**

a to remind readers to switch off their fans
b to entertain readers
c to explain how fans work
d to describe a character

10 Explain why the hairs on the back of Samuel's neck rose. **CRITICAL**

____

____

LESSON 111

Feral and Spam

Point of View

To identify point of view, we have to look at the way characters act and feel. The clues are in the way they express their opinions and views (what they think and feel).

Read the passage.

Put a box around the narrator's name.

I hate being a twin. I guess it might be OK if you were an identical twin. You could fool other people by pretending you were the other twin. But Sam and I only got the bad bits of being a twin—like having to share our birthday. That was a real drag.

"I'm not having a party with all of his friends there," I yelled.

"Now Fairlie," Mum began in her best 'don't-argue-with-me' voice, "I'm not having two separate birthday parties. I don't see why you make so much fuss about this."

Circle how Fairlie feels about being a twin.

Highlight pronouns that show who is telling the story.

Circle the correct answers.

1. From Fairlie's **point of view**, what is one of the worst things about being a twin?
   - a swapping identities
   - b sharing identities
   - c sharing birthdays
   - d sharing chores

2. Which phrase is the best **clue** to question 1's answer?
   - a having a party
   - b a real drag
   - c Sam and I
   - d the other twin

3. From whose **point of view** is the passage written?
   - a Fairlie's
   - b Sam's
   - c Mum's
   - d a friend's

4. Which pronouns helped you answer question 3?
   - a *you* and *your*
   - b *he* and *his*
   - c *I* and *our*
   - d *they* and *them*

5. Which word shows that Mum **thinks** Fairlie is overreacting?
   - a separate
   - b parties
   - c birthday
   - d fuss

AC9E4LY05 Use comprehension strategies to build inferred meaning

Read the passage.

Colour what Mum threatened to do.

"Perhaps I should just organise a party for Sam this year," Mum threatened.

"Yeah. Perhaps there should just be a party for Sam," Sam agreed.

"Fine," I said. "Suits me. Sam can have his party this year and I'll have mine next year."

Sam didn't look quite so happy with that idea. Mum did though.

"What a wonderful idea, Fairlie," she said.

"Wonderful," Sam said without enthusiasm.

Underline what Mum thought of Fairlie's idea.

Put a box around how Sam said "Wonderful".

6 What did Mum **think** of Fairlie's idea?

7 How did Sam **feel** when Mum suggested that this year's party be just for him?

8 How did Sam's **feelings** change when Fairlie suggested that they take turns in having a party?

9 Which phrase suggests that Sam did not really **think** that Fairlie's idea was so wonderful?

LESSON 112

Isabella

Cause and Effect

To find cause and effect, we ask why something happens and what the result is.

Read the passage.

Highlight the object Toby tripped over.

Underline the reason Toby dug through the sand.

Circle the object that was buried in the sand.

Toby climbed down the stairs to the beach. He looked out across the sea as he walked. Suddenly, Toby tripped over something and fell face first into the sand.

Toby stood up and brushed the wet sand from his clothes. He bent down for a closer look at what he had tripped on.

It was a piece of wood. As Toby lifted it, something underneath caught his eye. He dug through the sand and uncovered a bell. Toby lifted the bell and scraped off the barnacles. There was a date carved on its side.

"1892," Toby read.

Colour what was clinging to the bell.

Put a box around the date on the bell.

Circle the correct answers.

1. What **caused** Toby to trip?
   - a a bell
   - b a broken stair
   - c a hole in the sand
   - d a piece of wood

2. What **caused** Toby to dig through the sand? He …
   - a saw something.
   - b felt something.
   - c heard something.
   - d smelt something.

3. What **happened** when Toby dug through the sand? He found …
   - a some barnacles.
   - b a bell.
   - c a piece of wood.
   - d an old box.

4. What is the most likely **reason** the bell was covered in barnacles? It had once been …
   - a on a boat.
   - b in the ocean.
   - c on a rock.
   - d on dry land.

5. What **happens** when barnacles come in contact with a hard surface? They …
   - a try to eat it.
   - b swim around it.
   - c attach themselves to it.
   - d play with it.

AC9E4LY05 Use comprehension strategies to build literal and inferred meaning

Read the passage.

Put a box around the date in the diary.

Highlight who wrote the diary entry.

Colour the reason the lighthouse keeper fell asleep.

Circle what happened to the light that night.

Underline what happened to *The Isabella*.

Felix Thompson was seated at the table.

Felix stood and looked at Toby. "I'm sorry about before." Then he handed Toby a black book. "This is my great-grandfather's diary. It tells all about the night of 12 October 1892."

Toby was stunned. He opened the lighthouse keeper's diary and read. "It has been a bad week. Storm, after storm, after storm. I was dead on my feet. Fell asleep on watch. The light must have gone out during the night. I didn't know any damage had been done until the next day. When I heard that *The Isabella* was missing in my waters, I lied, when I filled in the logbook."

6 **Why** did Felix's great-grandfather fall asleep on the night of 12 October 1892?

7 What **happened as a result** of Felix's great-grandfather falling asleep that night?

8 What is the most likely **reason** that Felix's great-grandfather lied when he filled in the logbook?

LESSON 113

Caught in the Act

Visualisation

Visualising pictures of the people, places, things and events we are reading about helps build better understanding. Looking for key words in the text will help us create images that match the text.

Read the passage.

Underline the words and phrases that helped you see how the dragonfly approached the runway.

Colour the words and phrases that helped you see how Troy landed on the lily pad.

Highlight the words and phrases that helped you see how the green beetle arrived at the lily pad.

I couldn't believe it. The runway was a lily pad. We were going too fast. How would he stop in time? The lily pad seemed so small. Suddenly, the dragonfly stopped in midair. He hovered over the lily pad and dropped me. Luckily it was a soft landing.

"Do you have any idea how dangerous that is?" I yelled.

The dragonfly said nothing. He flew off, leaving me alone on the lily pad.

A small boat, made from a leaf, pulled up to the side of the lily pad.

"Are you Troy Cooper?" asked the green beetle who was driving the boat.

1. Read the passage again. As you do, visualise what you are reading about. Draw a picture of the images as you read about the events described in the passage.

Approaching the lily pad	Landing on the lily pad

Meeting the green beetle

AC9E4LY05 Use comprehension strategies such as visualising to build literal and inferred meaning

Read the passage.

Highlight the words and phrases that helped you see the ants taking Troy to the courtroom.

Underline the words and phrases that helped you see the courtroom.

The ants dragged me up the stairs and along a corridor. We came to a door, where another ant was standing guard.

"Is this Troy Cooper?" asked the guard.

"Yes, this is the accused," replied one of my captors.

The door opened. The courtroom was huge. All sorts of insects were seated around the walls. I wished I'd just wake up from this nightmare.

A bee stepped in front of a large platform. "All rise," he buzzed. "I introduce to you, the Honourable Judge William J. Moth."

Colour the words and phrases that helped you see the bee introducing the judge.

2 Read the passage again. As you do, visualise what you are reading about. Draw a picture of the images as you read about the events described in the passage.

The ants taking Troy to the courtroom

What Troy saw in the courtroom

The bee introducing the judge

AC9E4LY05 Use comprehension strategies such as visualising to build literal and inferred meaning

LESSON 114

Two Old Crows

Sequencing Events

To identify the sequence of events in a text, look at numbers and words that give clues to the order in which things happen.

Read the passage.

Circle where the crows sat.

Highlight the words that tell how the crows talked.

Two old crows sat on a fence rail.
Two old crows sat on a fence rail,
Thinking of effect and cause,
Of weeds and flowers,
And nature's laws.
One of them muttered, one of them stuttered,
One of them stuttered, one of them muttered.
Each of them thought far more than he uttered.
One crow asked the other crow a riddle.
One crow asked the other crow a riddle:
The muttering crow
Asked the stuttering crow,
"Why does a bee have a sword to his fiddle?"

Colour all the words that tell what the crows thought about.

Underline the question the crow asked.

Circle the correct answers.

1. In the passage, what is the **first** thing the two old crows do?
   - a fly to a fence
   - b sit on a fence
   - c think about nature
   - d talk to each other

2. What do the two old crows do **after** thinking of effect and cause? They think of …
   - a trees and bushes.
   - b grass and seeds.
   - c rivers and streams.
   - d weeds and flowers.

3. In the passage, what is the last thing that happens?
   - a One of the crows asks a riddle.
   - b One of the crows answers a riddle.
   - c One of the crows starts to mutter.
   - d One of the crows starts to stutter.

AC9E4LY05 Use comprehension strategies to build literal and inferred meaning

Read the passage.

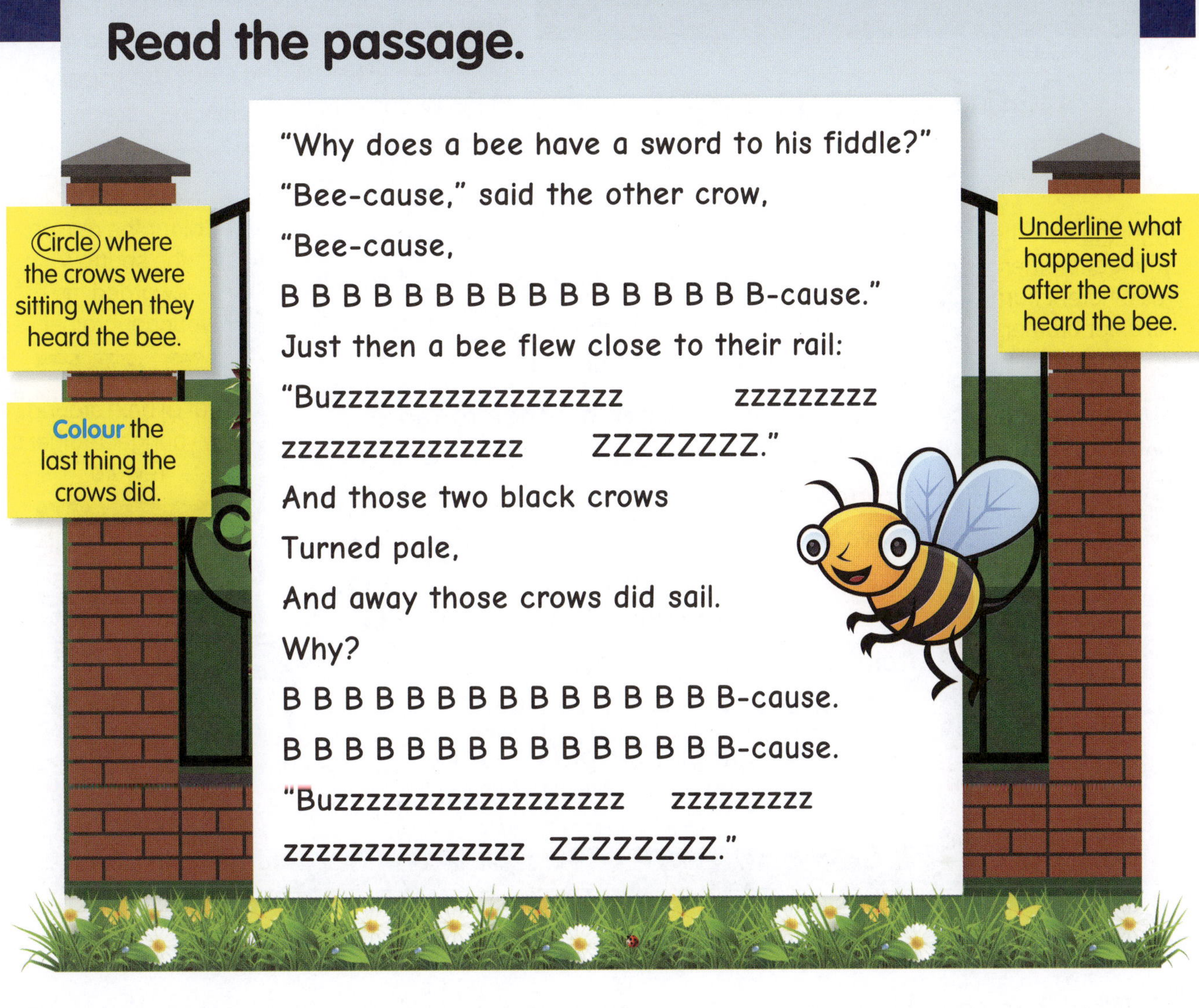

"Why does a bee have a sword to his fiddle?"
"Bee-cause," said the other crow,
"Bee-cause,
B B B B B B B B B B B B B B B B-cause."
Just then a bee flew close to their rail:
"Buzzzzzzzzzzzzzzzzzzz zzzzzzzzz
zzzzzzzzzzzzzzz ZZZZZZZZ."
And those two black crows
Turned pale,
And away those crows did sail.
Why?
B B B B B B B B B B B B B B B-cause.
B B B B B B B B B B B B B B B-cause.
"Buzzzzzzzzzzzzzzzzzzz zzzzzzzzz
zzzzzzzzzzzzzzz ZZZZZZZZ."

4 Complete the following sentences.

Two black crows were sitting on a **a** ______________________. Suddenly they heard **b** ____

____.

When they heard the bee, **c** ____

____.

They were scared the bee would sting them, so **d** ____________________________

____.

LESSON 115

Two Brothers, Two Rewards

Interpreting Character Behaviour, Feelings and Motivation

To interpret a character's feelings and why they act in a certain way, you need to look for clues in the text. The clues are usually in the words and punctuation.

Read the passage.

Underline how the younger brother was different from his older brother.

Highlight what the younger brother did when he found the injured sparrow.

Colour the reason the sparrow rewarded the younger brother.

Put a box around the younger brother's reward.

There were once two brothers who were very different from each other. The older brother, though rich, always wanted more. The younger brother was not rich, but he was happy with what he had.

One day the younger brother found a sparrow with a broken wing. He took it home and nursed it back to health. When it was time for the sparrow to fly away, it said, "You showed me great kindness, yet expected nothing in return. Please take this pumpkin seed. Plant it in your garden and wait for it to ripen."

When the pumpkins ripened, they contained gold, silver and diamonds.

Circle the correct answers.

1. What is the most likely reason the younger brother took care of the injured sparrow?
   - a He felt sorry for the sparrow.
   - b He expected the sparrow to reward him.
   - c He wanted the sparrow as a pet.
   - d He wanted to sell the sparrow.
2. Which adjective best describes the younger brother?
   - a greedy
   - b rich
   - c caring
   - d curious
3. Which two phrases in the passage are the clues to question 2's answer?
   - a took it home
   - b great kindness
   - c fly away
   - d nursed it
4. What is the most likely reason the sparrow rewarded the younger brother? The sparrow was …
   - a angry with the younger brother.
   - b grateful to the younger brother.
   - c scared of the younger brother.
   - d feeling generous.

AC9E4LY05 Use comprehension strategies to build literal and inferred meaning

Read the passage.

(Circle) the reason the older brother wanted the sparrow to get better quickly.

News of his brother's sudden fortune reached the older brother. When he heard what had happened, he took out a slingshot, shot a sparrow and broke its wing. He took the bird home and nursed it while thinking, "The sooner you are better, the sooner I get my reward."

When the bird was better, it gave the older brother a pumpkin seed. The seed sprouted into a vine, but the vine did not grow along the ground — it grew up into the sky. "I shall climb the vine and collect my reward," said the older brother.

He climbed the vine all the way to the moon. As soon as he stepped onto the moon, the vine disappeared.

Put a box around the reward the sparrow gave the older brother.

Colour what happened when the older brother got to the top of the vine.

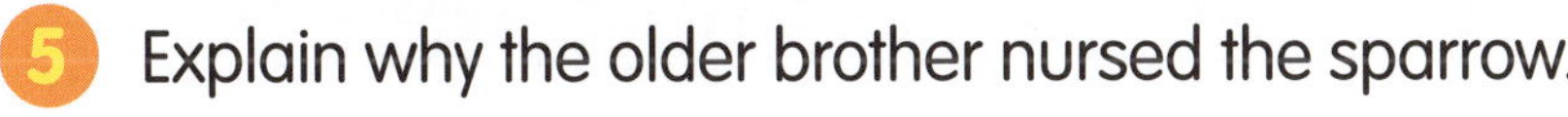

5 Explain why the older brother nursed the sparrow.

6 How do you think the sparrow **felt** when the older brother broke its wing?

7 Do you think the older brother got the reward he deserved? Give reasons.

GRAMMAR LESSON 3

Compound Sentences

A **compound sentence** contains **two or more main clauses**. The clauses are usually joined with the **conjunctions** ***and, but, or*** and ***so.*** For example: **Dogs can bark. They can howl. They can't talk. Dogs can bark and they can howl, but they can't talk.**

Read the extract.

In this sentence, circle **two conjunctions**.

In this sentence, **highlight three main clauses**.

In the last sentence, put a box around the **conjunction**.

In the last sentence, **colour** the **main clauses**.

Goat Girl and Garden Boy

Anula was very busy, but she wrote a letter to her mother every week and gave it to Aunty Padma to post. She included a return envelope and stamp each time, but so far her mother had not written back.

Aunty Padma gave Anula money for her school lunches and pocket money for the weekend, but Anula didn't spend the money. She saved it for her bus fare home.

In the meantime, Anula worked hard at her English, music and tennis lessons. She barely had time each evening to slip out of the house with the computer under her arm to visit her pet goat, Beni and her friend, Jegan.

Beni seemed content to remain in Jegan's room — until the day of the Spring Lawn Party. Aunty Padma had planned the party for months. She'd hired a caterer, and she'd invited all the important tea merchants.

Circle the correct answers.

In each of the following sentences, identify the conjunction.

1. Aunty Padma gave Anula money for her school lunches and pocket money for the weekend.
   a for b her c and d the
2. Aunty Padma gave Anula money for her school lunches, but Anula didn't spend the money.
   a for b but c didn't d the
3. Anula couldn't keep Beni in her room, so she asked Jegan to keep him.
   a couldn't b so c she d to
4. Anula could practise her music lesson, or she could play tennis.
   a or b she c could d her
5. Aunty Padma had planned the party for months and everyone was looking forward to it.
   a had b the c to d and

AC9E4LA04 Identify how text connectives are used to connect ideas

6 **Complete each sentence with a conjunction from the box.**

so	but	and	or

a Anula could stay with Aunty Padma, ____________ she could go home.

b Aunty Padma wanted Anula to stay ____________ Anula wanted to leave.

c Anula was worried about her goat, ____________ she asked Jegan to help her.

d Jegan kept the goat in his room ____________ fed it vegetables from the garden.

7 **In each sentence, underline the main clauses.**

a Beni had grown bigger, but he still fitted in the case.

b Anula was feeling lonely, so she wrote to her mother.

c Aunty Padma saw it all and then she fainted on the lawn.

d The boy grabbed Beni and dumped him into Anula's arms.

e Anula had enough money for two bus tickets, so Jegan could come too.

f Aunty Padma posted Anula's letters home, but she kept the ones that came back.

8 **In the following text, choose the correct word to fill each gap.**

Anula didn't know if she should leave her little goat, Beni, at home, **A** if she should take him with her to Aunty Padma's. It would be easier to leave him at home, **B** she would miss him so much! She decided to put him in her suitcase **C** nobody would see him. She poked holes in the suitcase **D** put Beni on top of her clothes.

A	○ but	○ and	○ or	○ so
B	○ and	○ or	○ so	○ but
C	○ so	○ but	○ and	○ or
D	○ but	○ and	○ so	○ or

AC9E4LA04 Identify how text connectives are used to connect ideas

LESSON 116

Antarctica

Word Study

We can often work out the meaning of words we do not understand by using clues in the text.

Read the passage.

Colour the object the meteorologists sent into the atmosphere.

Highlight three things the balloon recorded.

Research stations in Antarctica are busy places. A visitor might describe a typical day like this:

Early this morning I joined a group of meteorologists as they launched a weather balloon. The balloon rose high into the sky and recorded temperature, wind speed and air pressure. Scientists then studied the results.

After that, I watched a glaciologist drill ice cores. Ice cores contain air bubbles of gas from thousands of years ago. Glaciologists study the ice cores to learn more about the Earth's atmosphere.

Put a box around what the glaciologist was drilling.

Underline the reason glaciologists study ice cores.

Circle the correct answers.

1. What did the meteorologists send into the atmosphere?
   - a a hot air balloon
   - b a helium balloon
   - c a weather balloon
   - d a water balloon
2. What word can best replace the phrase *temperature, wind speed and air pressure*?
   - a tornadoes
   - b weather
   - c hurricanes
   - d snowstorms
3. Based on your answers to questions 1 and 2, what is the best definition of a meteorologist? Someone who studies how …
   - a weather affects the environment.
   - b balloons affect the environment.
   - c tornadoes form.
   - d snowstorms form.
4. What is a glacier? A slowly moving mass of …
   - a mud
   - b soil
   - c water
   - d ice
5. What does a glaciologist most likely study? All forms of …
   - a soil
   - b ice
   - c water
   - d mud

AC9E4LY05 Use comprehension strategies such as connecting to expand topic knowledge and ideas

Read the passage.

<u>Underline</u> what the geologists were doing.

Colour the information contained in the rock samples.

Research stations in Antarctica are busy places. A visitor might describe a typical afternoon like this:

After lunch, I flew by helicopter to where geologists were collecting rock samples. These contain important information about the Earth from millions of years ago.

Finally, I saw a marine biologist check the electronic tag that was glued to a Weddell seal. These tags record information about where marine animals travel in the ocean.

Highlight what the biologist was doing.

Circle the key word that helps us work out what the word *marine* means.

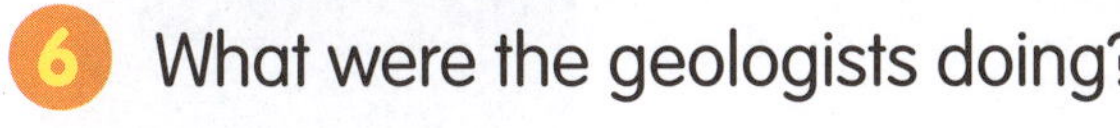

6 What were the geologists doing?

7 What information do the rocks contain?

8 Use your answers to questions 6 and 7 to help you write a description of what a geologist does.

9 What is a marine animal?

LESSON 117

Energy

Finding the Main Idea and Supporting Details

To discover what a text is about, you need to look for the main idea or key point. Facts and details in the text can help you find the main idea.

Read the passage.

Colour four things that can make electricity.

Circle the key word that tells how fuels such as coal can be turned into electricity.

Underline how sunlight is captured to make electricity.

Highlight what happens to water when it is heated.

Put a box around the verb that tells how steam powers a turbine.

The most common way to make electricity is to burn a fuel, such as coal. This heats water to make steam. The steam spins a turbine. This powers a generator to make electricity.

There are other ways to make electricity. Wind and water can also power a generator. A solar cell absorbs sunlight to make electricity.

Electrical energy can be converted into other forms of energy, such as heat, light and sound.

Lightning is an electrical current that jumps through the air. The current heats the air hotter than the surface of the sun.

Circle the correct answers.

1. What is the **main idea** or **key point** of the passage?
   - a why electricity is made
   - b how electricity is made
   - c where electricity is made
   - d when electricity is made

2. Which three **details** best **support the main idea**?
   - a Lightning is an electrical current that jumps through the air.
   - b Electricity is made by burning coal.
   - c A solar cell absorbs sunlight to make electricity.
   - d Electrical energy can be converted into heat.
   - e Wind and water can power a generator to make electricity.

AC9E4LY05 Use comprehension strategies to build literal and inferred meaning

Read the passage.

<u>Underline</u> what potential energy is.

Colour what kinetic energy is.

(Circle) an example of potential energy.

Put a [box] around an example of kinetic energy.

Work waiting to be done is potential energy. Work being done is kinetic energy.

Potential energy is energy that could be released or used. A coiled spring has potential energy because the spring could uncoil. A rock on the edge of a cliff has potential energy. Its potential energy is the energy that would be released if it fell from the cliff.

The food we eat becomes potential energy when it is stored in our bodies. When this energy is used to do things, such as kick a ball, it becomes kinetic energy.

3 What is the passage **mainly** about? ____________________

4 List at least three **details** that **support the main idea**.

a ____________________

b ____________________

c ____________________

LESSON 118

The Arctic

Identifying Audience and Purpose

To identify the author's purpose, it helps to work out who the text was written for. The language the author uses will show what his or her purpose is — to inform, persuade, instruct, or entertain. For example, texts about scientific subjects will contain lots of technical and scientific words.

Read the passage.

Underline why many countries argue over who owns the Arctic.

Colour the reason Russian scientists researched the land beneath the Arctic Ocean.

The countries that make up the Arctic often argue about who owns it. Many countries want the Arctic's valuable oil and gas deposits.

In 2007, 50 Russian scientists used a mini submarine to research the seabed under the North Pole. They were trying to prove that the land underneath the Arctic Ocean is connected to their land in Siberia. They even planted a Russian flag on the seabed.

There are over 10 billion barrels of oil and natural gas deposits in the Arctic territory. Canada, Norway and Greenland are also trying to prove that they own the land under the Arctic waters.

Highlight how much oil and natural gas there is in the Arctic.

If you don't know what the term *oil and gas deposits* means, put a **W** next to it. If you know what the term means, put a ✓ next to it.

Circle the correct answers.

1. What is the author's **main purpose** in writing this text?
   - a to persuade readers that Russia owns the land beneath the Arctic waters
   - b to inform readers about the countries that are trying to prove ownership of the Arctic
   - c to entertain readers with stories about the Arctic

2. Who is the **target audience** for this text?
   - a scientists
   - b politicians
   - c oil and gas companies
   - d the general public

3. What is the **clue** to question 2's answer? The author uses language that …
   - a most people can understand.
   - b only scientists can understand.
   - c only politicians can understand.
   - d only adults can understand.

AC9E4LY03 Identify the characteristic features used in imaginative, informative and persuasive texts to meet the purpose of the text

Read the passage.

Underline the definition of an igloo.

Colour what size the blocks of snow should be.

Circle all the verbs that give orders.

An igloo is a dome-shaped shelter, made out of blocks of snow.

What you need:

- A snow saw
- Dry snow

What to do:

1. Use the saw to cut blocks of hard, dry snow, about one metre long and 20 centimetres deep.
2. Draw a circle in the snow and stand in the middle of it. Place the blocks around the circle in layers. The blocks of snow should overlap and lean towards the centre.
3. Place the last block on top of the igloo. Cut it to fit the hole.
4. Cut a tunnel under the wall for the entrance. Poke small breathing holes in the walls.

Highlight the instruction that tells how to form the blocks of snow into a dome shape.

Put a box around the key word that tells how people will enter and leave the igloo.

4 What is the purpose of the text?

5 List six verbs that helped you work out the answer to question 4.

6 Who would be most likely to build an igloo?

7 Do you think that people who live in places where it doesn't snow would be interested in reading the text? Give one or more reasons for your answer.

8 Based on your answer to question 4, who is the **target audience** for the text?

LESSON 119

Advertisements

Visualisation

Visualising pictures of the people, places, things and events we are reading about helps to build better understanding. Looking for key words in the text will help us create images in our heads.

Read the passage.

Circle the words that helped you see what kind of service the advertiser offers.

Highlight the words that helped you see what the advertiser's quotes are based on.

Underline the words that helped you see what other jobs the advertiser does.

It's summer—let us mow your lawn! Our fast, on time lawn mowing service always does a great job. Long list of happy customers, who enjoy professional work with a smile. Free quotes based on the size of your lawn, how many trees in it and how overgrown it is for the first mow. We also do yard cleanups, weed removal and gutter clearing. No job too big or small.

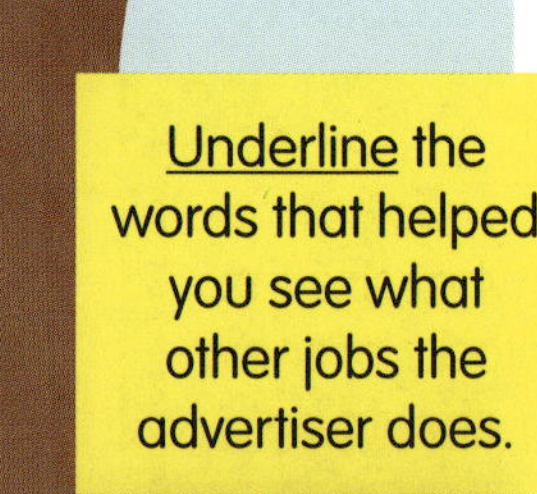

1. Read the passage again. As you do, visualise what you are reading about. Draw a picture of the images you create as you read about some of the things in the advertisement.

The kind of service the advertiser offers

Other jobs the advertiser does

What the advertiser's quotes are based on

AC9E4LY05 Use comprehension strategies such as visualising to build literal and inferred meaning

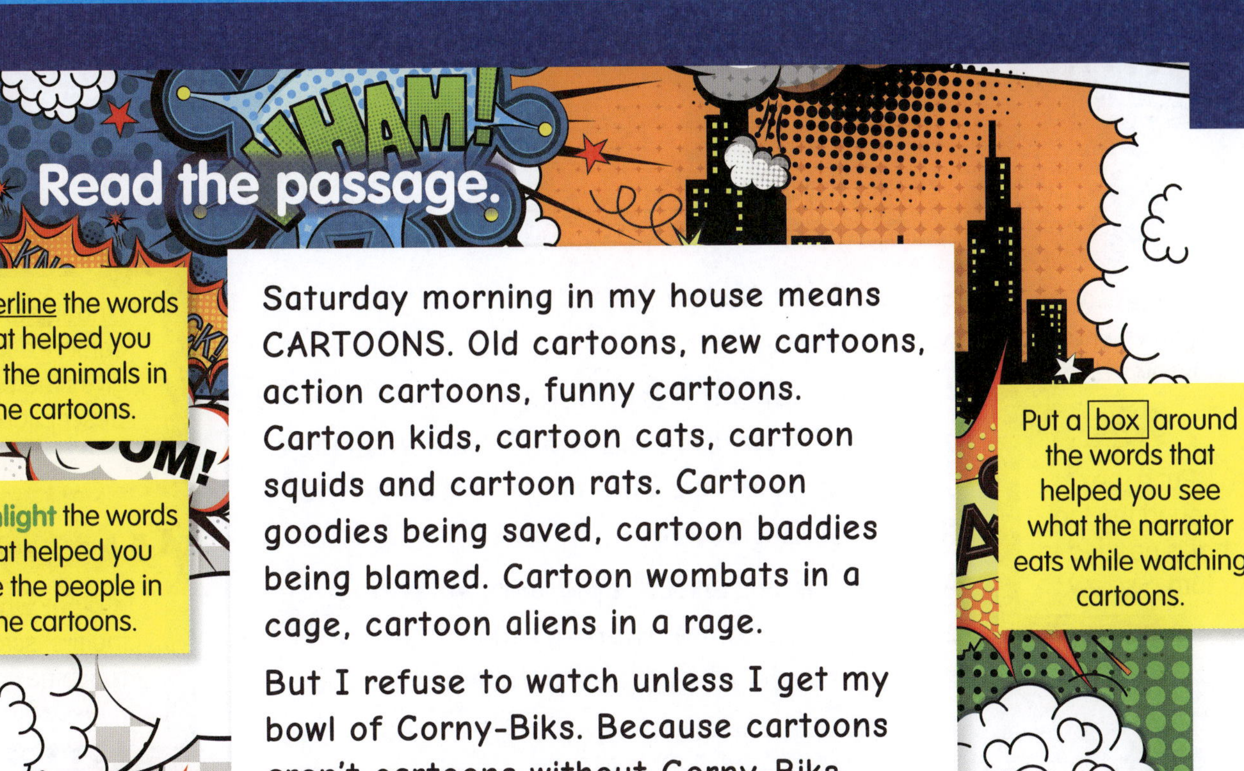

Read the passage.

Underline the words that helped you see the animals in the cartoons.

Highlight the words that helped you see the people in the cartoons.

Saturday morning in my house means CARTOONS. Old cartoons, new cartoons, action cartoons, funny cartoons. Cartoon kids, cartoon cats, cartoon squids and cartoon rats. Cartoon goodies being saved, cartoon baddies being blamed. Cartoon wombats in a cage, cartoon aliens in a rage.

But I refuse to watch unless I get my bowl of Corny-Biks. Because cartoons aren't cartoons without Corny-Biks.

Put a box around the words that helped you see what the narrator eats while watching cartoons.

2 Read the passage again. As you do, visualise what you are reading about. Draw a picture of the images you create as you read about some of the things in the advertisement.

Cartoon animals

Cartoon people

Narrator eating breakfast

LESSON 120

Simple Machines

Important Information

To find the most important information in a text, we need to look for the words, phrases or sentences that tell us the most about the subject.

Read the passage.

Circle three verbs that tell what screws do.

Put a box around the tool that is needed to turn a screw.

Screws hold things together, and lower and raise things.

A screw is an inclined plane wrapped around a cylinder. The inclined plane forms a ridge along the cylinder. This ridge is called the thread of the screw.

As a screw is turned by a screwdriver, it turns a greater distance than it moves forward. The turning motion becomes a forward motion.

A Greek mathematician called Archimedes invented a screw machine more than 2200 years ago. It was used to lift water into fields and out of ships.

Underline the sentence that gives the best description of a screw.

Colour what the first screw machine was used for.

Circle the correct answers.

1 Which **three** sentences tell how a screw works?

a Screws hold things together, and lower and raise things.

b A screw is an inclined plane wrapped around a cylinder.

c The inclined plane forms a ridge along the cylinder.

d This ridge is called the thread of the screw.

e As a screw is turned by a screwdriver, it turns a greater distance than it moves forward.

f Some screws work by lowering and raising things.

g A Greek mathematician called Archimedes invented a screw machine more than 2200 years ago.

2 Of the three sentences you chose in question 1, write out the one you think best sums up what screws are used for.

____

____

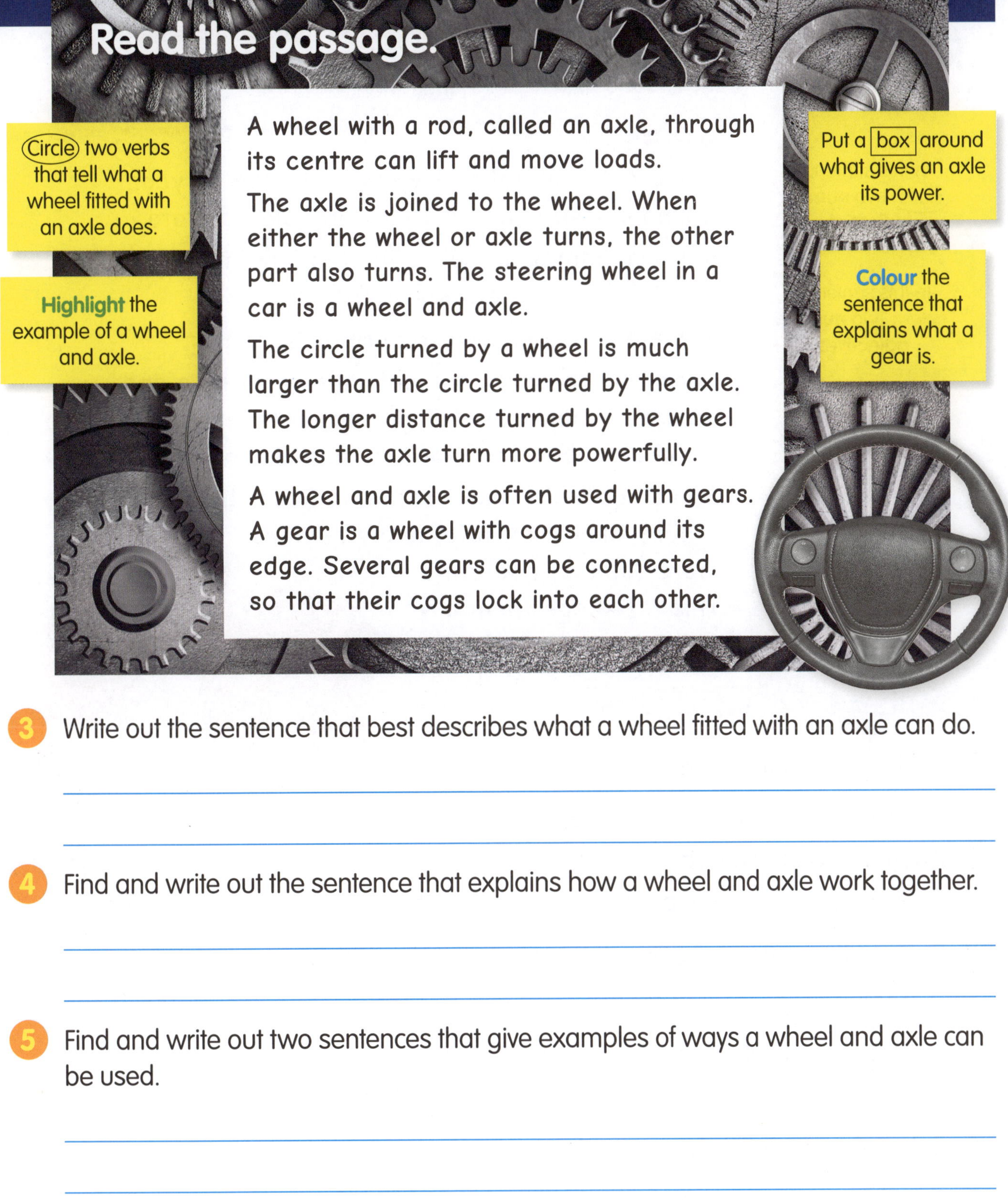

Read the passage.

A wheel with a rod, called an axle, through its centre can lift and move loads.

The axle is joined to the wheel. When either the wheel or axle turns, the other part also turns. The steering wheel in a car is a wheel and axle.

The circle turned by a wheel is much larger than the circle turned by the axle. The longer distance turned by the wheel makes the axle turn more powerfully.

A wheel and axle is often used with gears. A gear is a wheel with cogs around its edge. Several gears can be connected, so that their cogs lock into each other.

Circle two verbs that tell what a wheel fitted with an axle does.

Highlight the example of a wheel and axle.

Put a box around what gives an axle its power.

Colour the sentence that explains what a gear is.

3 Write out the sentence that best describes what a wheel fitted with an axle can do.

4 Find and write out the sentence that explains how a wheel and axle work together.

5 Find and write out two sentences that give examples of ways a wheel and axle can be used.

Determiners

A **determiner** comes before a common noun. It can be:

- an **article** (**a, an, the**)
- a **number adjective** (**two, many, all, some**)
- a **pronoun** that points out a noun (**this hat, these books, that car, those bikes**)
- a **possessive pronoun** (**my house, his toy, their friends**)

Read the extract.

In this sentence, circle two **number adjectives**.

In this sentence, colour two **number adjectives**.

In this sentence, put a box around the **article**.

In the last sentence, highlight the **pronoun** that points out a noun.

Cold

Some cold habitats have snow and ice all year. Animals have adapted to live in cold habitats.

Many mammals in cold climates have two layers of fur. This keeps them warm and dry.

Some animals hibernate during the winter.

During hibernation, the animal's heart rate and breathing slow down. Their body temperature drops. It takes a long time for the animals to wake up.

Some squirrels, mice, bats and bears hibernate. Before they hibernate, many animals store food as body fat. This fat keeps them alive while they hibernate.

Circle the correct answers.

In the following sentences, identify the determiner.

1. Animals like brown bats hibernate during the winter.
   a like   b brown   c the   d during
2. During hibernation, an animal's heart rate and breathing slow down.
   a heart   b an   c and   d down
3. During hibernation, their body temperature drops.
   a their   b body   c During   d temperature
4. Before those animals hibernate, they store food as body fat.
   a they   b as   c animals   d those
5. During winter, many animals stay warm in dens and burrows.
   a in   b and   c many   d animals

AC9E4LA06 Understand that complex sentences contain one independent clause and at least one dependent clause typically joined by a subordinating conjunction to create relationships, such as time and causality

6 **Complete each sentence with a determiner from the box.**

all	an	less	its	That	Every	the	a

a The hedgehog is feasting on __________ earthworms.

b Not __________ animals hibernate during cold weather.

c There is __________ food for animals in the cold winter months.

d Whales have __________ thick layer of blubber to keep them warm.

e __________ year, animals travel long distances to warmer climates.

f __________ hedgehog has made __________ nest in __________ old box .

7 **Circle the word that correctly completes each phrase.**

a	_____ icy wind	a	an
b	_____ humpback whales	a	the
c	_____ large bears	this	these
d	_____ hibernating animals	much	more
e	_____ little mouse	that	those
f	_____ interesting animals	one	some

8 **Choose the correct word to fill each gap.**

Winter is **A** coldest season. In **B** places it gets very cold. **C** plants stop growing in winter. **D** animals spend **E** time sleeping in winter.

A	◯ a	◯ an	◯ the	◯ those
B	◯ one	◯ some	◯ each	◯ much
C	◯ A	◯ This	◯ Every	◯ Most
D	◯ Any	◯ Many	◯ That	◯ An
E	◯ more	◯ few	◯ other	◯ its

ASSESSMENT 2:

The Time Keepers

Lexile: 780

Clocks have been ticking away the time for centuries. The oldest clock in existence today is in a cathedral in England. It is over 700 years old.

Many early clocks had no hands and no faces. They told time simply by striking the hour. Bells were an important part of these clocks. In fact, the word clock comes from the French word, *cloche*, meaning 'bell'.

Early clocks relied on a falling weight to turn wheels inside the clock to tick away the time. They were not good time keepers. They could lose or gain half an hour to two hours a day.

The first hand to be introduced was the hour hand. Often it did not move. Instead, the numbers marked on the face of the clock moved. The minute hand was introduced when a pendulum replaced the falling weight and after that, time keeping became more reliable. Later, a spring replaced the pendulum in many clocks. A key was used to wind the spring inside the case and it would slowly unwind to tick away the time. A second key wound a spring that struck a bell every hour. Time keeping became much more accurate.

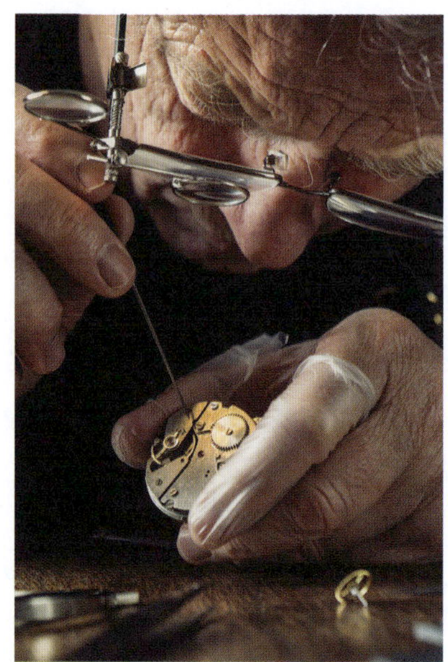

The first watches appeared about 500 years ago. Some early watches struck the hours, but most had to be watched—hence the name, watch.

Once, all clocks and watches were handmade. Nowadays, they are made by machines in factories. There are all sorts of watches—pocket watches, wrist watches, digital watches and stop watches. There are all sorts of wall, mantel and desk clocks. There are digital clocks, clocks with alarms, cuckoo clocks, electric clocks and grandfather clocks.

Circle the correct answers.

1 When did people first start using clocks? **LITERAL**

a 700 years ago

b less than 700 years ago

c more than 700 years ago

d 70 years ago

2 Where is the world's oldest existing clock? LITERAL

a in a castle in England
b in a cathedral in England
c in a museum in England
d in a country house in England

3 How were early clocks different from later ones? Early clocks … INFERENTIAL

a had no faces or hands.
b were made of wood.
c were accurate time keepers.
d were made in factories.

4 Why is it helpful for people to know the time? Choose the best answer. Knowing the time helps people … CRITICAL

a relax.
b sleep at night.
c organise their lives.
d lead healthier lives.

5 What is a pendulum? VOCABULARY

a a pointer
b a type of key
c a swinging weight
d a type of watch

6 How did the introduction of the pendulum affect time keeping? It made time keeping … LITERAL

a more accurate.
b less accurate.
c more complicated.
d more interesting.

7 Nowadays, clocks and watches are made by machines in factories. This has resulted in an increase in the … CRITICAL

a number of clocks and watches.
b price of clocks and watches.
c quality of clocks and watches.
d size of clocks and watches.

8 In the text, what is a spring? VOCABULARY

a a sudden movement
b a coil of wire
c a change in the weather
d a type of well

9 In what way are all clocks and watches similar? They all … INFERENTIAL

a have minute and hour hands.
b make sounds.
c tell the time.
d look the same.

10 How did the watch get its name? LITERAL

____

____

LESSON 121

Kevin's Echidna

Figurative Language

Similes and metaphors are examples of figurative language. They use comparisons to help us visualise pictures. Similes compare one thing to something else using the words *like* or *as*. Metaphors make a more direct comparison. They do not use *like* or *as*.

Read the passage.

Highlight the objects the echidna's quills are compared to.

Colour the objects the hairs on the echidna's face are compared to.

Kevin could see the echidna so clearly—its black-tipped, creamy quills, as sharp as knitting needles; the coarse, black hairs on its face, like bristles on a brush; its eyes, two beads shining against the dull blackness of its snout.

Put a box around the objects the echidna's eyes are compared to.

Circle the correct answers.

1. Which **two** figures of speech are **similes**?
   - a the coarse, black hair of its face, like bristles on a brush
   - b the dull blackness of its snout
   - c its eyes, two beads
   - d quills as sharp as knitting needles

2. Which **two** words helped you identify the **similes**?
   - a as
   - b on
   - c against
   - d like

3. What picture of the hairs on the echidna's face does the **simile** give us? The hairs on the echidna's face are ...
   - a long.
   - b beautiful.
   - c prickly.
   - d colourful.

4. Which figure of speech is a **metaphor**?
   - a like bristles on a brush
   - b sharp as knitting needles
   - c the dull blackness of its snout
   - d its eyes, two beads

5. What picture of the echidna's eyes does the **metaphor** give us? The echidna's eyes are ...
   - a small and bright.
   - b big and dull.
   - c oval and grey.
   - d round and watery.

AC9E4LE04 Examine the use of literary devices and deliberate word play in literary texts to shape meaning

Read the passage.

Circle the object Kevin's legs are compared to.

Highlight the objects the leaves are compared to.

Kevin climbed to the highest branch of the tree and balanced there. His legs had turned to stone, but he forced himself to look down. Brown leaves were floating on the murky water, like little boats. He took a deep breath and plunged into the pool. It wasn't the greatest dive he had ever done, but as he surfaced, the fear was gone.

6 The writer says Kevin's legs had turned to stone. What figure of speech is this?

7 What do you think the writer is telling us when he compares Kevin's legs to stone?

8 Do you think this is a good way to describe how Kevin was feeling? Why, or why not?

9 The writer compares the brown leaves to little boats. What figure of speech is this?

10 Do you think this is a good way of describing the leaves? Why, or why not?

LESSON 122

Buzz, the Computer Man

Interpreting Character Behaviour, Feelings and Motivation

To interpret a character's feelings and why they act in a certain way, you need to look for clues in the text. The clues are usually in the words and punctuation.

Read the passage.

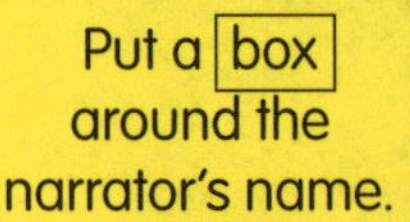

Put a box around the narrator's name.

Underline what Samantha said to Lisa.

Circle the punctuation that helps to show that Samantha was angry.

Colour how Samantha planned to get back at Lisa.

"If I win the map-a-thon," said Lisa, "I don't want to take Samantha to Wonderland. I want to take Sarah." Sarah is Lisa's best friend.

I couldn't believe that Lisa wouldn't want to take me. She knew how much I wanted to go to Wonderland. I didn't keep it a secret.

"You're the meanest person I know!" I told her. "It would serve you right if someone else won the tickets to Wonderland."

I decided I would do my best to try to win. Then I'd take one of my friends instead of Lisa.

I grabbed her atlas and went to my bedroom to study.

Circle the correct answers.

1. How did Samantha **feel** when Lisa said she wanted to take Sarah to Wonderland?
   a pleased b confused c upset d excited

2. What is a **clue** to question 1's answer? Samantha accused Lisa of being …
   a a liar. b lazy. c a cheat. d mean.

3. Which **punctuation** helps to answer question 1?
   a . b , c ! d "

4. Why did Samantha decide to study for the map-a-thon? She wanted to …
   a win the map-a-thon. b take one of her friends to Wonderland.
   c help Lisa win. d show Lisa how clever she was.

AC9E4LY05 Use comprehension strategies to build literal and inferred meaning

Read the passage.

Highlight the words that show that the narrator was scared of Ram.

Circle two words that show that Ram was angry.

Underline the words that Buzz used to praise Ram.

Put a box around what Ram did after Buzz praised him.

When Ram saw me, he stopped shouting. I hid behind Buzz, trying to make myself as small as possible.

Ram frowned. He loomed over Buzz. "Do you know the penalty for bringing an outsider into the computer?" he roared.

Buzz nodded. "But I was hoping you would see this as a special case," Buzz said, "and show a little kindness to a poor girl who needs the help of your great, almighty wisdom."

Ram stopped frowning and began to smile a little.

Buzz told Ram about the map-a-thon and the trouble that I'd been having. I needed something to help me remember the names of countries, and cities, and especially of oceans and seas.

5 Why might the narrator have tried to make herself as small as possible?

6 Which words suggest that Ram was angry with Buzz?

7 Carefully explain how Buzz made Ram smile.

8 Do you think that Ram will help the narrator? Give a reason for your answer.

LESSON 123

The Creaky House Club

Identifying Audience and Purpose

To identify the author's purpose in writing a text, it helps to work out who the text was written for. The language the author uses will show what his or her purpose is — to inform, persuade, instruct, or entertain. For example, texts that contain dialogue and lots of descriptive words might be telling a story.

Read the passage.

In paragraph 1, circle two adjectives that describe how Sam was feeling.

Highlight the adjective that shows how Sam felt about keeping a secret from his friend.

Underline the dialogue in the passage.

At home, Sam looked at the kitchen clock. One hour to go. Part of him was excited but the rest of him was terrified. What if the club members did something really bad to him? Something where they didn't mean to hurt him, but it went wrong?

Sam knew there was no way out of it. He had to show up. He just wished that Tristan was coming too. He felt rotten about keeping it all from his friend. How was he going to tell Tristan if he did get into the Creaky House Club?

"I'll see you later, Dad," Sam called, as he left the house and cycled towards The Creaky House.

Circle the correct answers.

1. Which option best describes this text? It is part of …
   - a an explanation.
   - b a story.
   - c a diary entry.
   - d a set of instructions.
2. Based on your answer to question 1, what is the main purpose of the text?
   - a to inform
   - b to persuade
   - c to warn
   - d to entertain
3. What can we **infer** about Sam and Tristan? Sam and Tristan are …
   - a at preschool.
   - b kindergartners.
   - c in primary school.
   - d at university.
4. Who is the most likely audience for this text?
   - a under 5's
   - b adults
   - c 8–12-year-olds
   - d cyclists

AC9E4LY03 Identify the characteristic features used in imaginative, informative and persuasive texts to meet the purpose of the text

Read the passage.

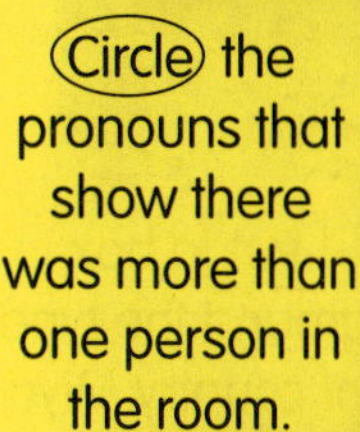

Circle the pronouns that show there was more than one person in the room.

Colour the word that helps us work out how old the boys were.

Highlight the informal expression Sam uses for *made a mistake*.

A voice that sounded familiar said, "Welcome to The Creaky House Club, Sam. As you know, we select our members very carefully. Firstly, we'd like to know why you want to join our club."

Sam had thought they'd ask him this question, but he still didn't have a good answer.

"Well ... I'm a good basketball player and I'd like to be part of the most popular group in school at the moment," said Sam.

"At the moment?" came the reply. "What do you mean 'at the moment'?"

"I've goofed already," Sam thought. But aloud he said, "Well, at the moment and in the future I mean."

5 Who is Sam talking to? ________________

6 What does the dialogue suggest about the kind of text this is?

7 What is the main reason authors write these types of text?

8 Who do you think the target audience is for this text? Give a reason/s for your answer.

LESSON 124

The Woman and the Corn

Making Inferences

To make inferences while reading, we have to use clues in the text. The clues help us find the answers that are hiding in the text.

Read the passage.

Underline who Miya's father was.

Highlight what the voice offered to do.

Narrator: Once upon a time, there lived a young woman called Miya. Her father was lord of his people. One day, Miya was swimming in the river when she heard a voice.

Miya: What was that? Who's there?

Narrator: A voice from the sky asked her to follow it through the jungle.

Miya: Sure, I've got some spare time...but as long as I'm home before dark.

Narrator: So Miya followed the voice as best she could through the jungle until she reached a cave.

Put a box around the type of country Miya travelled through.

Circle the correct answers.

1. What **inference** can we make about the voice? It belonged to …
   - a the man of Miya's dreams.
   - b someone Miya couldn't see.
   - c Miya's father.
   - d an animal.

2. What is the **clue** to question 1's answer? In the text it states that Miya followed …
   - a the man.
   - b the woman.
   - c the shadowy figure.
   - d the voice.

3. What **inference** can we make about what Miya mainly saw on her way to the cave? Miya most likely saw lots of …
   - a trees.
   - b deserts.
   - c mountains.
   - d oceans.

4. Which word is the **clue** to question 3's answer?
   - a cave
   - b jungle
   - c dreams
   - d voice

AC9E4LY05 Use comprehension strategies to build inferred meaning

Read the passage.

Underline the reason Jose came to see Miya.

Colour the welcome the villagers gave Miya.

Narrator: One day Jose, a farmer from Miya's village, appeared at the cave.

Jose: Miya? Miya? Are you there? There is a famine and we have no food. We are starving. Help us!

Miya: *<to Lord of the Bats>* My husband, I love you but I must leave and return to my village. The villagers need me.

Narrator: So Miya and Jose returned to their village, but Miya did not receive a hero's welcome.

Miya's father: Stop right there! We are hungry because of you, Miya. It is your fault we have no corn.

Narrator: Miya was very upset and returned to the Lord of the Bats.

Lord of the Bats: Don't cry, Miya, because you can still help your village. This is what you must do.

Highlight what Miya's father said to her.

Put a box around how Miya felt after her father spoke to her.

5 What can we **infer** about the kind of person Miya is? Support your answer with evidence from the text.

6 Why might Miya's father have blamed his daughter for the famine?

7 What can we **infer** about the kind of person the Lord of the Bats is? Support your answer with evidence from the text.

LESSON 125

The Young Lion King

Important Information

To find the most important information in a text, we need to look for the words, phrases or sentences that tell us the most about the subject.

Read the passage.

Underline the reason Lion King did not think Fox would make a good teacher.

Highlight the reason Lion King did not choose Mole.

Lion King wondered which animal could teach the Lion Prince. He wondered if Fox could do it. Fox, though clever, was a great liar and liars always cause trouble. He wondered about Mole. Mole was orderly and careful but never looked far ahead. The King wondered about Panther. Panther was strong, brave and a great fighter, but liked fighting a little too much. The Lion knew that a good king is just, wise and can solve things without fighting.

Put a box around the things Lion King liked about Panther.

Colour the reason Lion King did not want Panther to teach Lion Prince.

Circle the correct answers.

1. Which three animals did Lion King think of when looking for a teacher for the Lion Prince?

   a Fox b Panther c Wolf

   d Mole e Bear f Snake

2. Which three sentences give the most information about why Lion King **did not** choose those animals?

   a He did not think Fox could do it.

   b Fox, though clever, was a great liar and liars always cause trouble.

   c He wondered about Mole.

   d Mole was orderly and careful but never looked far ahead.

   e The King wondered about Panther.

   f Panther was strong, brave and a great fighter, but liked fighting a little too much.

AC9E4LY05 Use comprehension strategies to build inferred meaning

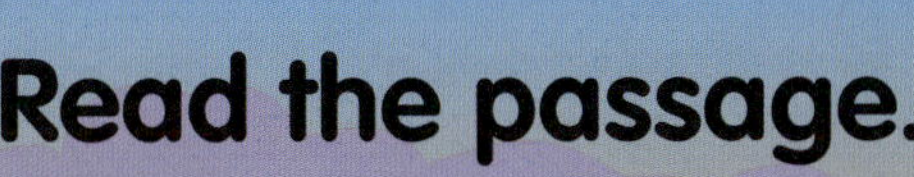

Read the passage.

Circle the animal Lion King chose to teach his son.

Highlight what the Lion Prince had learnt.

Lion was still thinking when Eagle flew by. "Of course!" Lion cried. "Eagle!" The Lion King sent his son to study at Eagle's court.

Years later, Lion Prince returned to his father, in time to take over his kingdom.

"Father," said the Lion Prince, "I have learnt many things. I can tell where every bird can find water. I know what kind of food each bird needs. I know how many eggs it lays and the wants of every bird that flies. When I am in charge of the kingdom, I shall begin to teach our animals how to build nests."

The animals in the King's court howled with laughter. The King realised the Lion Prince had not been taught the knowledge a great king needs most of all — a knowledge of the wants and needs of his own people and land.

Colour what the other animals did when they heard what Lion Prince had learnt.

Underline the information that the Lion Prince needed most of all.

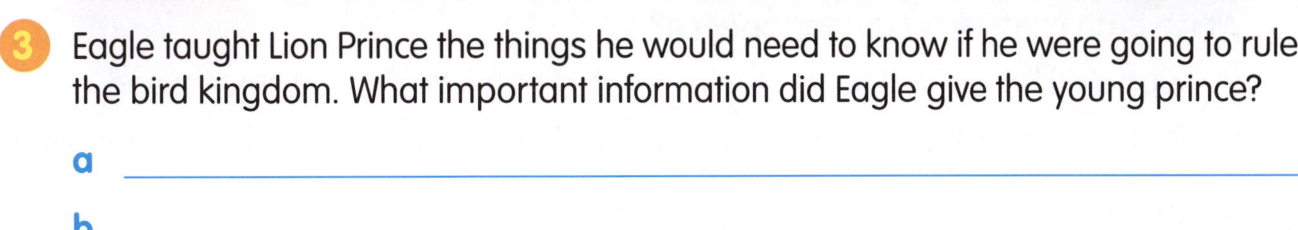

3. Eagle taught Lion Prince the things he would need to know if he were going to rule the bird kingdom. What important information did Eagle give the young prince?

a ______________________________

b ______________________________

c ______________________________

d ______________________________

4. What should the Lion Prince have learnt?

____

____

____

____

GRAMMAR LESSON 5

Quoted and Reported Speech

Quoted speech repeats the exact words someone says. **Quotation marks** (" ") are placed around the speaker's words, **including any punctuation**. For example: **Molly said, "I want to bake a cake."**

Reported speech tells what someone said. Speech marks are not used. For example: **Molly said she wanted to bake a cake.**

Read the extract.

In paragraph 1, underline the exact words Suan said to his friend.

In paragraph 2, colour what Pedro asked his friend.

In paragraph 3, highlight what Pedro told Suan.

In paragraph 4, put a box around what Pedro asked Suan.

How Suan Became Rich

Pedro and Suan were friends. Pedro had inherited a great fortune, but Suan was as poor as the poorest beggar. Early one morning Suan went to his friend and said, "Do you have some wood that you do not need?"

"Yes, I do," said Pedro. He asked his friend what he needed the wood for. Suan replied that he wanted to build a house.

Pedro gave Suan the wood. He told him not to worry about paying for it.

Suan, who had not thought evil of his friend, took the wood and built his house. When it was finished, his house was much better than his friend's house. This made Pedro so angry that he asked Suan to give back the wood.

Circle the correct answer for each question.

1 Which is an example of **quoted speech**?

- a Suan said he needed some wood.
- b Suan said, "I need some wood."
- c Suan asked his friend for some wood.
- d Suan said that he wanted some wood.

2 Which is an example of **reported speech**?

- a Pedro said he had some wood.
- b Pedro said, "I have some wood."
- c Pedro said, "Don't pay for it."
- d Pedro said, "Give me back the wood."

3 Which word can be left out of the following sentence without changing its meaning?
Suan said that he was going to build a house.

- a going
- b a
- c was
- d that

4 *Pedro said Suan could have the wood.* Which sentence is closest in meaning?

- a Pedro said, "I have some wood."
- b "This is his wood," said Pedro.
- c Pedro said, "You can have the wood."
- d Pedro said, "You must take the wood."

AC9E4LA12 Understand that punctuation signals dialogue through quotation marks and that dialogue follows conventions for the use of capital letters, commas and boundary punctuation

5 Correct each sentence by writing the underlined verb in the past tense.

a Suan said his friend <u>is</u> ______________ not evil.

b She said she <u>wants</u> ______________________ a house like his.

c They said they <u>do</u> ______________ not want to live in a wooden house.

d The boy said he <u>likes</u> ______________________ his new house.

e The builders said they <u>are</u> _________________ waiting for the bricks.

f He said he <u>will</u> _________________ give him wood for his house.

g The man said he <u>can</u> ______________________ deliver the wood.

6 Write each sentence as reported speech.

a The builder said, "I need more bricks."

The builder said he ____

____

b The man said, "I am going to buy the house."

The man said he ____

____

c "The house is too small," complained the woman.

The woman complained that ____

____

d Suan said, "I will replace all of the wood."

Suan said he ____

____

e The girl said, "I want yellow walls in my room."

The girl said she ____

____

AC9E4LA12 Understand that punctuation signals dialogue through quotation marks and that dialogue follows conventions for the use of capital letters, commas and boundary punctuation

LESSON 126

Forces

Compare and Contrast

When we compare and contrast information, we look for the similarities and differences between details in the text.

Read the passage.

Circle the cause of earthquakes, wind and waves.

Underline what happens when plates push against each other and pull apart.

Highlight what happens to warm air.

Colour the words that show the difference between earth tremors and earthquakes.

Forces cause earthquakes, wind and waves in and on the Earth.

The Earth's surface is made up of large, slow-moving plates of rock. The plates push against each other and pull apart. This releases energy, which causes the land above the plates to move. This might be an earth tremor that you can't feel or a violent earthquake.

Wind is caused by changes in air pressure. When warm air rises, cooler, heavier air rushes in to fill the space. This moving air is called wind.

Ocean waves are caused by the force of the wind.

Circle the correct answers.

1. How are earth tremors and earthquakes **similar**? Both are caused by …
   - a changes in air pressure.
   - b moving plates of rock.
   - c violent winds.
   - d the earth's gravitational pull.
2. How are earth tremors and earthquakes **different**? Earth tremors are …
   - a stronger than earthquakes.
   - b louder than earthquakes.
   - c weaker than earthquakes.
   - d bigger than earthquakes.
3. How are wind and waves **similar**? Both are caused by …
   - a pushing and pulling apart.
   - b changes in air pressure.
   - c slow-moving plates of rock.
   - d gravity.
4. How are warm air and cool air **different**? Warm air is …
   - a dirtier than cool air.
   - b thicker than cool air.
   - c saltier than cool air.
   - d lighter than cool air.

Read the passage.

Underline the force that sends the ball towards the net.

Circle the force that slows the ball down.

Colour the force that pulls the ball down.

When a basketball player shoots, a push force sends the ball towards the net. Friction with the air slows the ball down. Gravity pulls it back towards the court. The ball would just keep going up without the action of these forces.

An aircraft has four forces acting on it. The engines produce a forward force, called thrust. The wings produce an upward force called lift. Friction from air rushing over the aircraft, called drag, slows it down. Gravity pulls it towards the earth.

What happens to an object depends on the sum of all the forces acting on it. The basketball reaches the net because the force of the shot is greater than the effects of gravity and friction. The aircraft moves forward because the thrust from the engines is greater than gravity and drag.

Highlight the force produced by an aircraft's wings.

Circle the force that slows the aircraft down.

Colour the force that pulls the aircraft down.

5 Which force causes both the ball and the aircraft to slow down?

____

____

6 Which force causes both the ball and the aircraft to return to Earth?

____

____

7 Explain the reason:

a the basketball reaches the net. ______________________________

____

b the aircraft moves forward. ______________________________

____

LESSON 127

People and the Sea

Making Inferences

To make inferences while reading, we have to use clues in the text. The clues help us find the answers that are hiding in the text.

Read the passage.

Underline the main reason people set sail in early times.

Circle what people used to think the Earth looked like.

Colour the reasons some ships sank.

From early times people have set sail on the oceans to explore the unknown. Some explorers looked for new lands to settle. Others looked for fame, treasure or adventure.

Long before science helped us understand the oceans, people thought the Earth was flat. Sailors believed that if they sailed far enough, they would fall off the edge of the world. Of course they never did, but storms, pirates and hidden reefs meant that some ships did sink to the bottom of the sea. Today, adventurers go in search of sunken treasure!

Circle the correct answers.

1 What can we **infer** about early explorers?

a They all wanted to find new lands.
b They all hoped to find treasure.
c They went to sea for different reasons.
d They all found fame and fortune.

2 Which two words are the best **clues** to question 1's answer?

a *explore* and *unknown*
b *Some* and *Others*
c *lands* and *settle*
d *sail* and *oceans*

3 What can we **infer** about some of the old ships that sank?

a They contained treasure.
b They were steam ships.
c They fell off the edge of the world.
d They didn't sail far enough out to sea.

4 Which sentence is the best **clue** to question 3's answer?

a Others looked for fame, treasure or adventure.
b Some explorers looked for new lands to settle.
c Sailors believed that they would fall off the edge of the world.
d Today, adventurers go in search of sunken treasure!

AC9E4LY05 Use comprehension strategies to build inferred meaning

Read the passage.

Circle the different methods of catching fish.

Highlight the different uses of seaweed.

Underline the sentences that give information about the amount of fish caught today.

People have always caught fish and other sea creatures using baskets, hooks and nets. Today large fishing boats can catch, clean and freeze fish while still at sea.

Modern fishing boats take huge amounts of seafood from the sea. Popular ocean fish that people eat include tuna, herring, sardines, cod and snapper. Every year about 75 million tonnes of fish are caught worldwide.

Seaweed is also harvested. People eat it raw or cooked and sometimes use it to thicken foods such as ice-cream and yoghurt. Seaweed can also be used to make toothpaste and sausages!

5 We can **infer** that there are different methods of catching fish. What evidence is there in the text to support this statement?

6 We can **infer** that more fish are caught today than were caught in the past. What evidence is there in the text to support this statement?

7 Based on the information in paragraph 3, what can we **infer** about seaweed?

LESSON 128

Architecture

Finding Facts and Information

To find facts and information in a text, we usually ask the questions **Who? What? Where?** or **When?** The answers can be clearly seen in the text.

Read the passage.

Circle what many famous buildings become.

Highlight the number of entries the State Government received.

Put a box around the name of the winning entrant.

Underline the winning entrant's nationality.

Colour the date work on the Sydney Opera House began.

Highlight where in Sydney the Opera House stands.

Many famous buildings become icons. The Sydney Opera House has become an icon of Australia.

In 1955, the NSW State Government decided that Sydney needed an opera house. It wanted one of the world's great buildings, so it ran a competition. There were 233 design entries from 32 countries.

The winner was Jøern Utzon, a Danish architect. He worked with Ove Arup, an English civil engineer. Work began in March 1959 at Bennelong Point on Sydney Harbour.

Circle the correct answers.

1 According to the text, **what** do many famous buildings become?

a ruins b tourist attractions c icons d world heritage sites

2 **Who** designed the Sydney Opera House?

a Ove Arup b Jøern Utzon

c the NSW State Government d the Australian Government

3 From **how many** entries was the winner of the competition chosen?

a 232 b 32 c 233 d 323

4 **Where** did the winning architect come from?

a Denmark b Australia c England d the United States

5 **When** did work on the Sydney Opera House begin?

a in 1955 b in 1995 c in 1963 d in 1959

AC9E4LY05 Use comprehension strategies to build literal meaning

Read the passage.

Underline what an architect thinks about when designing a building.

Circle the name of the architect of *Fallingwater*.

Highlight the year that *Fallingwater* was designed.

An architect thinks about the land, and where it is, when designing. This is called responding to the site.

Fallingwater is a house famous for the way its design responds to its site. It was designed by an American architect, Frank Lloyd Wright, in 1935.

The site was owned by Edgar Kaufmann. It had a stream and a waterfall. Kaufmann thought Wright would design a house with a view of the waterfall. Instead, Wright placed the house right over the waterfall. He told Kaufmann, "I'm designing a building to the music of the stream."

Put a box around the nationality of the architect who designed *Fallingwater*.

Colour the words that tell where the architect placed *Fallingwater*.

6. **What** does an architect think about when designing a building?

____

____

____

7. **Who** designed *Fallingwater*? ______________________

8. **When** did the architect design *Fallingwater*? ______________________

9. **Where** did the architect who designed *Fallingwater* come from? ______________

10. Explain **how** the architect responded to the site when designing *Fallingwater*.

____

____

____

____

LESSON 129

How Big Is Your Carbon Footprint?

Cause and Effect
To find cause and effect, we ask why something happens and what the result is.

Read the passage.

Underline the reason many scientists say temperatures are rising.

Highlight where ice is melting.

Circle the cause of the melting ice.

Almost all scientists believe that we should be concerned about global warming. Firstly, they say measurements taken on Earth and in space show that the average temperature is getting higher. They attribute this rise in temperature to the gases released into the atmosphere when fossil fuels are burned. Secondly, the warmer temperatures are causing vast chunks of ice to melt around the north and south poles, resulting in rising sea levels. This could lead to coastal areas and low-lying land being swamped.

Finally, they point to the shrinking of glaciers in many parts of the world.

Colour what could happen if sea levels continue to rise.

Put a box around how rising temperatures are affecting glaciers.

Circle the correct answers.

1. According to many scientists, what is **causing** temperatures to rise?
   - a storms on the sun
   - b earthquakes and volcanoes
   - c disappearing rainforests
   - d burning fossil fuels
2. According to many scientists, what **effect** are gases from burning fossil fuels having on the earth? They are **causing** …
   - a temperatures to fall.
   - b temperatures to rise.
   - c lots of thunderstorms.
   - d earthquakes and volcanoes.
3. What **could happen** if sea levels continue to rise?
   - a Swamps will form.
   - b The land will rise with the water.
   - c Coastal areas will be swamped.
   - d The continents will break up.
4. What do many scientists believe is **causing** glaciers to shrink?
   - a rising temperatures
   - b heavy rainfall
   - c not enough rainfall
   - d strong winds

AC9E4LY05 Use comprehension strategies to build literal and inferred meaning

Read the passage.

Highlight the key phrase that tells us what some people believe about global warming.

Underline what some people blame global warming on.

But some people believe that global warming is a natural process that has been happening for the last 6 000 years. The average temperature today, they say, is approximately 11 degrees warmer than it was back then, but it has been rising gradually since that time, not suddenly in the last 100 years. These people blame global warming on the way our planets are aligned and the effect they have on our orbit, and that is something we have no control over.

I don't buy those arguments – I believe the science. I have always preferred to err on the side of caution, so I will continue to switch off lights and do whatever I can to reduce my carbon footprint on the planet.

Colour what the author is going to continue doing.

5 Carefully explain what some people believe is the **cause** of global warming.

6 What **effect** does the author believe his or her actions might have on the environment?

LESSON 130

Coral Reefs

Word Study

We can often use clues in the text to help us work out the meaning of words we do not understand.

Read the passage.

Underline words that explain what camouflage is.

Colour the reason some fish change colour.

Put a box around the reason some predators change colour.

Many reef fish have bright colours. This provides them with good camouflage. Colourful spots and stripes make them difficult to see among the coral. Some fish can even change their colour to hide from predators. Others, such as trumpetfish, are predators that change colour to trick their prey.

Circle the correct answers.

1. Which **best** describes what camouflage is?
   - a scales
   - b a disguise
   - c colour
   - d speed
2. Which phrase is the **clue** to question 1's answer?
   - a bright colours
   - b Colourful spots and stripes
   - c trick their prey
   - d make them difficult to see
3. Which **best** describes a predator?
   - a a hunter
   - b a victim
   - c an old fish
   - d a large fish
4. What are the **two best clues** to question 3's answer? Some fish …
   - a have to hide from predators.
   - b have bright colours.
   - c are predators that change colour to trick their prey.
   - d have good camouflage.

5. Which word in the passage is the **opposite** of predator?
   - a fish
   - b spots
   - c trick
   - d prey

AC9E4LY05 Use comprehension strategies such as connecting to expand topic knowledge and ideas

Read the passage.

Highlight words that help us work out the meaning of *fragile*.

Colour what happens when there are no longer any trees to protect the ground.

Underline how ships damage coral.

Coral reefs are fragile and they need to be protected. There are some natural threats to coral reefs, but people cause the most damage.

Coral needs clear water to grow. When forests are cut down on land, erosion washes soil into the ocean. The plants inside the corals stop growing and the corals begin to die.

Pollution caused by industry and shipping can also poison coral polyps. Ships leak fuel into the water and boat anchors break off coral. Oil spills can cause huge damage as well.

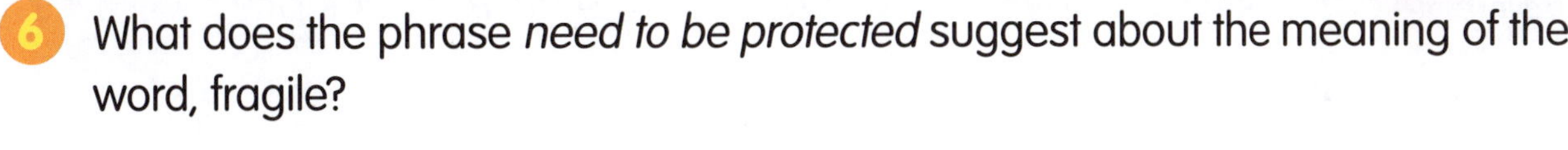

6. What does the phrase *need to be protected* suggest about the meaning of the word, fragile?

____

____

____

7. Use the **clues** in paragraph 2 to help you write a definition for erosion.

____

____

____

8. Use the **clues** in paragraph 3 to help you write a definition for pollution.

____

____

____

GRAMMAR LESSON 6

Fronted Adverbials

An **adverbial** is a word or phrase that tells ***where***, ***when*** or ***how*** an action happens. For example: **near the school, in a minute, carefully.** A **fronted adverbial** is an adverbial that comes at the beginning of a sentence. It is usually followed by a **comma**. For example: **A long time ago, dinosaurs roamed the Earth.**

Read the extract.

Saint Patrick's Day

Saint Patrick's Day began as a celebration of an Irish saint. Today it is a celebration of Ireland itself.

In this sentence, underline the **fronted adverbial.** → More than 1500 years ago, Patrick introduced Christianity to Ireland. He became Ireland's patron saint.

In this sentence, highlight the **adverbial phrase.** → In the seventeenth century, Irish people began celebrating Saint Patrick's Day. Families went to a church service. They also ate a big meal together.

In this sentence, put a box around the **adverb.** → Today, Saint Patrick's Day celebrates the history and culture of Ireland. People hold street parades and eat Irish food. They sing and dance to Irish music. Everything is coloured green, the unofficial colour of Ireland.

In the last sentence, circle the **fronted adverbial.** → Saint Patrick's Day is celebrated in more countries than any other national day. In America, the Chicago River is dyed green on Saint Patrick's Day.

Circle the correct answer for each question.

Each sentence starts with a fronted adverbial. After which word should there be a comma?

1 In Ireland people celebrate Saint Patrick's Day on 17 March.
a people b In c Ireland d on

2 About 400 years ago Irish people began celebrating Saint Patrick's Day.
a years b ago c people d About

3 On Saint Patrick's Day many Irish people wear something green.
a Day b many c Patrick's d people

4 After his death many legends grew up around Saint Patrick.
a up b legends c After d death

5 In Chicago the river is dyed green on Saint Patrick's Day.
a river b green c Chicago d the

AC9E4LA08 Understand how adverb groups/phrases and prepositional phrases work in different ways to provide circumstantial details about an activity

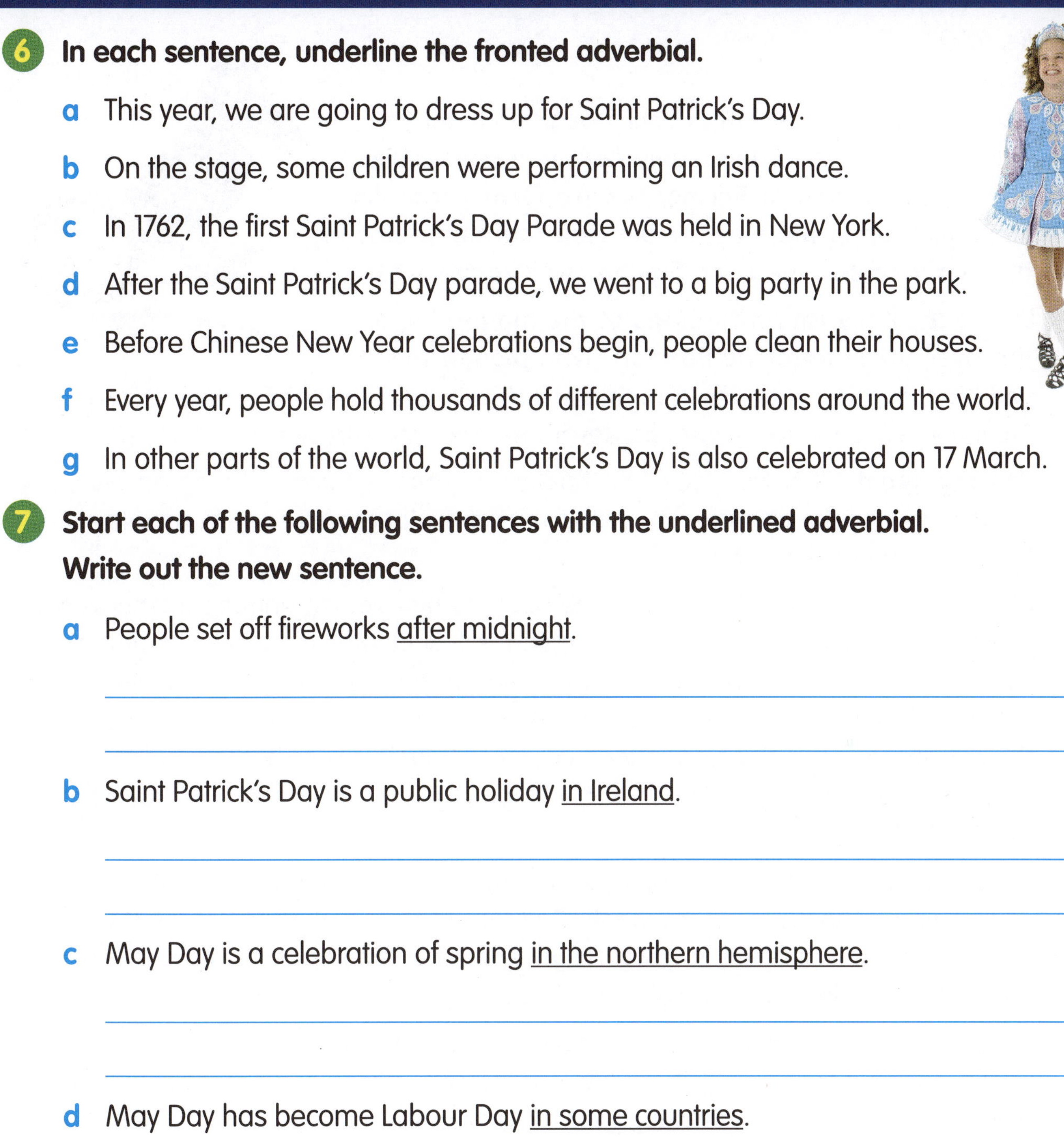

6 In each sentence, underline the fronted adverbial.

a This year, we are going to dress up for Saint Patrick's Day.

b On the stage, some children were performing an Irish dance.

c In 1762, the first Saint Patrick's Day Parade was held in New York.

d After the Saint Patrick's Day parade, we went to a big party in the park.

e Before Chinese New Year celebrations begin, people clean their houses.

f Every year, people hold thousands of different celebrations around the world.

g In other parts of the world, Saint Patrick's Day is also celebrated on 17 March.

7 Start each of the following sentences with the underlined adverbial. Write out the new sentence.

a People set off fireworks after midnight.

____

____

b Saint Patrick's Day is a public holiday in Ireland.

____

____

c May Day is a celebration of spring in the northern hemisphere.

____

____

d May Day has become Labour Day in some countries.

____

____

e Halloween is celebrated in many countries around the world on 31 October.

____

____

ASSESSMENT 3:

The Crow

Lexile: 760

Kelly is a black crow with a sharp beak and shiny feathers. He lives in a scraggly nest in a hollow tree, right in the middle of Farmer Flynn's farm. From his home high up in the tree, he can see the mountains in the distance and the river flowing away to the west.

But today Kelly isn't interested in the mountains or the river. He is watching Farmer Flynn plough the paddock, turning over the rich, black soil in long, straight furrows. When the farmer passes by, Kelly swoops down low over the furrows.

"What a feast I'll have today," he thinks. He follows Farmer Flynn on his tractor and pecks at the juicy grubs that the ploughshares turn up. How fresh and tasty they are!

After he has eaten his fill, Kelly flies back to his tree to snooze in the warm afternoon sun. When he wakens, the sun is low in the west. Kelly remembers the delicious meal he ate earlier and looks down at the newly-ploughed ground. He blinks when he sees something shining in the furrow. Curious, he flies down and lands nearby, then sidles cautiously towards the object. He gives it a peck. He jumps back in fright as it begins to make a noise—tick, tick, tick, tick.

Kelly stares at the yellow object for a long time. Then he pecks at it again ... and again. He shakes it in his beak. Suddenly the yellow thing wraps itself around his leg. Now Kelly is really frightened! He flies back to his tree with the yellow, ticking thing hanging from one leg.

Kelly perches on a branch and pecks at his enemy again and again. Eventually it loosens its grip on his leg and falls down into the hollow of his tree. He can still hear it ticking, but he is free at last. Kelly flies around his tree, squawking triumphantly.

Many months later, Farmer Flynn is mowing the grass near Kelly's tree. He stops to have lunch in its cool shade. As he is eating, he notices something shining in the hollow of the tree. He reaches in and pulls out a gold chain.

"Stars and bananas!" he exclaims. "It's my old pocket watch. Now how did it get here?"

Circle the correct answer for each question.

1 Where is Kelly's nest? LITERAL

a in a tree on a mountain
b in a tree on a farm
c in a tree beside the river
d in a tree in the city

2 Why would Farmer Flynn be ploughing the paddock? CRITICAL

a to make it look neater
b to destroy the grubs
c to get rid of the weeds
d to prepare it for planting

3 Which word in the text is similar in meaning to 'sleep'? VOCABULARY

a blinks
b swoops
c snooze
d wakens

4 When does Kelly notice the watch? LITERAL

a when he is feasting on grubs
b while watching Farmer Flynn
c when the sun is going down
d before he dozes off

5 The pocket watch is described as being shiny and yellow. This suggests that it is made of … INFERENTIAL

a silver.
b stainless steel.
c gold.
d plastic.

6 Why is Kelly frightened of the pocket watch? Choose the TWO best answers. CRITICAL

a It is a strange shape.
b It is shiny and yellow.
c It makes a strange noise.
d It wraps itself around his leg.

7 How long does Farmer Flynn's pocket watch lie in the hollow of Kelly's tree? LITERAL

a several months
b several years
c a few days
d two weeks

8 Which words best describe Farmer Flynn's feelings when he finds his pocket watch? INFERENTIAL

a surprised and puzzled
b surprised and annoyed
c disappointed and confused
d curious and worried

9 What is the main purpose of this text? CRITICAL

a to give information about crows
b to tell a story
c to explain how pocket watches work
d to describe a farm

10 What is the most likely reason Farmer Flynn's pocket watch was in the furrow? CRITICAL

On Our Way to Alpha Centauri

Making Connections

Linking a text to events in your own life is a great way to build understanding. Look for key words and phrases in the text to make the connections.

Read the passage.

Underline the words that describe Sarah's new home.

From now on Sarah's home would be a large, travelling space station. The shuttle was taking them to the big mother ship, Star Wanderer. It would carry all three hundred of them towards Alpha Centauri, and a lifetime of new discoveries.

Suddenly Sarah was scared. It was such an unknown future that lay ahead — like it was for those sailors, hundreds of years ago, sailing over the edge of a flat Earth.

Circle a feeling you most likely have experienced.

Put a box around the word that refers to the time ahead.

Circle the correct answers.

1 Which of the following have you experienced?

- a living on a space station
- b moving to another home
- c making new discoveries
- d travelling on a space shuttle
- e feeling scared
- f sailing on the ocean
- g wondering what the future holds
- h travelling somewhere with lots of other people

2 Which of the following is it possible you will experience in the future?

- a embark on exciting adventures
- b sail over the edge of a flat Earth
- c travel in outer space
- d sail around the world

AC9E4LY05 Use comprehension strategies such as connecting to expand ideas

Read the passage.

Underline a sentence that suggests that the people celebrating Christmas are not on Earth.

Circle the object that Sarah considers to be the most important part of Christmas.

"We've all left a lot behind us," started Sarah, and many faces grew serious. Dr. Singh was worried. Was Sarah going to remind them too much of earthly celebrations?

"For me, the most important part of Christmas is the Christmas tree. Every year I'd dream about what it would look like. I couldn't wait until it was time to start decorating it." Sarah continued, "Kapil and I have something special that comes from Earth. Something from the past to take us into the future."

Sarah signalled to Kapil, who tugged a cord.

The curtain fell. In front of them was a young apple tree, holding its branches and green leaves high. Seven red apples hung from the branches.

Highlight who helped Sarah prepare the Christmas surprise.

Colour the phrase that describes the tree.

Sarah, Kapil and the other people on the spaceship are celebrating their first Christmas away from Earth.

3. Write a paragraph describing a celebration, such as your birthday, Halloween or a religious holiday, that you have especially enjoyed. What did you do? What did you eat? Were there any decorations? Did you receive any presents? Who shared the celebration with you?

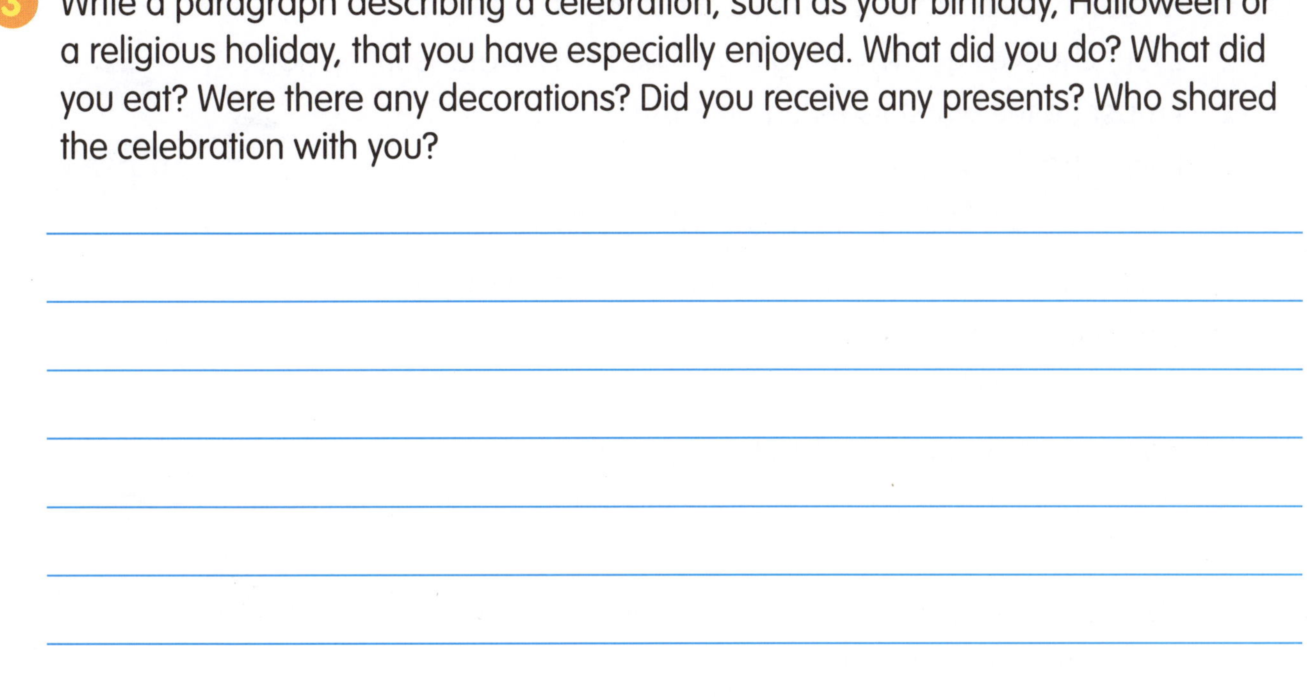

LESSON 132

Lure

Making Inferences

To make inferences while reading, we have to use clues in the text. The clues help us find the answers that are hiding in the text.

Read the passage.

Circle the adjective the narrator uses to describe the kind of fisherkid she is.

Underline the sentence that shows that the narrator likes to spend her free time fishing.

Highlight two sentences that suggest the narrator knows a lot about fishing.

I must be the worst fisherkid on Earth!

It isn't that I don't try. Every chance I get, I'm dangling a line in the water somewhere. My bookshelves are full of every fishing book and fishing map ever printed. I buy the best fishing line pocket money can buy. And I watch all the fishing reports on TV and listen to them on the radio as well.

Circle the correct answers.

1. What can we **infer** about the narrator?
   - a She hates fishing.
   - b She likes eating fish.
   - c She loves fishing.
   - d She wants to give fishing a try.
2. Which sentence is the best **clue** to question 1's answers?
   - a Every chance I get, I'm dangling a line in the water somewhere.
   - b I must be the worst fisherkid on Earth!
   - c It isn't that I don't try.
   - d I buy the best fishing line pocket money can buy.

3. What can we **infer** about the number of fish the narrator catches?
   - a She always catches lots of fish.
   - b She sometimes catches lots of fish.
   - c She never catches any fish.
   - d She often catches a few fish.
4. Which sentence is the best **clue** to question 3's answer?
   - a Every chance I get, I'm dangling a line in the water somewhere.
   - b It isn't that I don't try.
   - c I buy the best fishing line pocket money can buy.
   - d I must be the worst fisherkid on Earth!

AC9E4LY05 Use comprehension strategies to build inferred meaning

Read the passage.

Underline the words that describe the place where the fishermen went missing.

Colour the name of the place where the men went missing.

The fishing report suddenly becomes very serious. The reporter is warning people about the dangers of fishing from a popular local spot. Two fishermen have gone missing. The camera zooms in on the spot where the fishermen were last seen.

I know the spot — it's called Devil's Rocks. It's a good spot to catch kingfish. Suddenly, a huge wave comes out of nowhere and crashes over the rocky ledge.

Highlight words that show that the narrator is watching television.

Put a box around the words that suggest that Devil's Rocks is near the ocean.

5 We can **infer** that people often visit the spot where the two fishermen went missing. What is the **clue**?

6 The reporter warns that it could be dangerous to fish from the spot where the two men went missing. What other **clue** is there to **suggest** that this is a dangerous spot?

7 We can **infer** that the narrator is watching the fishing report on television. What are the **clues**?

8 What **evidence** is there to **suggest** that the spot where the men were fishing is near the ocean?

LESSON 133

Bush-wacked

Word Study

To identify the descriptive verbs in a text, look for the verbs that tell us exactly how an action is performed; for example, 'raced' instead of 'ran'. Descriptive verbs are effective because they help us visualise the actions.

Read the passage.

Circle the verb that is similar in meaning to stood up.

Highlight the verb that creates a picture of someone moving slowly and carefully.

Leaving the brilliant sunshine, it took a while for his eyes to adjust to the inky blackness. The hairs on the back of his neck bristled. Unaware that he was holding his breath, Spook inched forward, his shoes scraping on the earth. His fists were clenched. His fingernails bit into his palms.

The cave was narrow inside. Cobwebs veiled the walls like gauze.

Put a box around the verb that creates a picture of a creature sinking its teeth into flesh.

Underline the verb that creates a picture of something soft and filmy.

Circle the correct answers.

1 Which **verb** in the passage is similar in meaning to moved?

a bristled b scraping c inched d clenched

2 Why is the **verb** you chose in question 1 more effective than "moved"? It creates a picture of how …

a awkwardly Spook moved. b slowly and carefully Spook moved.
c quickly Spook moved. d smoothly and gracefully Spook moved.

3 Which of the following words from the text is **not a descriptive verb**?

a clenched b bit c bristled d was

4 Which **verb** in the passage is similar in meaning to covered?

a veiled b bristled c clenched d was holding

5 Why is the **verb** you chose in question 4 more effective than "covered"? It creates a picture of how …

a thick and rough the cobwebs were. b thin and delicate the cobwebs were.
c sticky and dirty the cobwebs were. d messy and broken the cobwebs were.

AC9E4LE04 Examine the use of literary devices and deliberate word play in literary texts, including poetry, to shape meaning

Read the passage.

Circle the verb that is similar in meaning to ran.

Highlight the verbs that suggest that the branches and thorns were attacking the boys.

Feet barely contacting the ground, the boys bolted—chased by the scream. Spook was in the lead, then Nathan and, well behind, Aaron, his short legs hardly able to keep pace. Branches and thorns stabbed and snatched at them. Long grass tickled their legs like creepy crawlies.

Eventually, out of breath, the trio stopped. They doubled over and gasped for air and their legs ached.

Colour the verb that lets us imagine what the grass felt like on the boys' legs.

Underline the verb that shows that the boys were taking short, quick breaths.

6 Which **descriptive verb** has the author used in place of "ran"?

7 What **picture** of the thorns do the **verbs** "stabbed" and "snatched" create?

8 The author writes that the long grass tickled the boys' legs. What **picture** does the **verb** "tickled" create?

9 What does the **verb** "gasped" **suggest** about the way the boys were breathing?

AC9E4LE04 Examine the use of literary devices and deliberate word play in literary texts, including poetry, to shape meaning

LESSON 134

The Opal Miner

Visualisation

Visualising pictures of the people, places, things and events we are reading about helps build better understanding of the text. Looking for key words in the text will help us create the images that match the text.

Read the passage.

Circle the words that helped you imagine what the desert looks like.

The Opal Miner

In the harsh and brittle desert
In a world of arid air
The rainbow's bending arch
Is magical and rare.

Highlight the words that helped you imagine what the rainbow looks like.

Put a box around the word that tells you that you won't often see a rainbow in the desert.

1 Read the poem again. As you do so, visualise what you are reading about. Draw a picture of the images you create of the desert and the rainbow.

The desert

The rainbow

AC9E4LY05 Use comprehension strategies such as visualising to build literal and inferred meaning.

Read the passage.

(Circle) the words and phrases that helped you imagine what the tunnels look like.

The Opal Miner

In the tunnels far below it
In a world of stubborn stone
The miner probes and follows
Strange visions of his own.

The miracles he dreams of
Far from dust and heat
Are glowing rainbow fragments
Underneath his feet.

Highlight the words and phrases that helped you imagine what the miner does in the tunnels.

Put a [box] around a phrase that helped you imagine what the opals look like.

2 Read the poem again. As you do so, visualise what you are reading about. Draw a picture of the images you create of the miner in the tunnels.

The miner in the tunnels	The miner seeing visions of opals in the rock

LESSON 135

The Eagle and the Spider

Compare and Contrast

When we compare and contrast information, we look for the similarities and differences between details in the text.

Read the passage.

Circle the clue to how Eagle reached the top of the mountain.

Highlight how Spider moved above Eagle's head.

Underline what Spider did when he was above Eagle's head.

Put a box around how Eagle thought Spider had reached the top of the mountain.

"How lucky am I," said Eagle, "that I have such powers of flight to take me so high and so far. There is no mountain too high for me! Here I am, looking down on all the world from a height no other living creature has ever reached!"

"What a boaster you are," said Spider, from a nearby twig. "Look where I am sitting. It isn't so far below you, is it?" Spider jumped to another twig, just above Eagle's head. He began to busily spin a web, just above Eagle.

"How did you reach this height?" asked Eagle. "You are weak and wingless. Did you somehow manage to crawl all the way up here?"

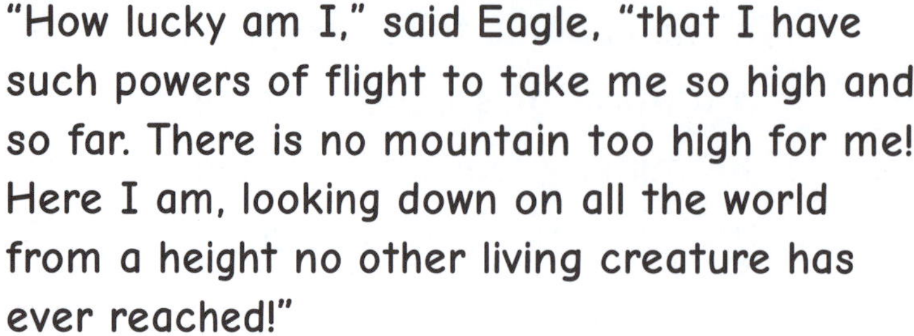

Circle the correct answers.

1. In what way are Eagle and Spider **similar**? Both are …
   - a birds.
   - b animals.
   - c insects.
   - d mammals.
2. In what way are Eagle and Spider **different**? Only …
   - a Spider can fly.
   - b Spider can hop.
   - c Eagle can fly.
   - d Eagle can run.
3. What can Spider do that Eagle can't?
   - a spin a web
   - b flap its wings
   - c build a nest
   - d soar above the earth
4. Which of the following sentences is **true**?
   - a Spider is bigger than Eagle.
   - b Spider is stronger than Eagle.
   - c Eagle is shorter than Spider.
   - d Eagle is heavier than Spider.

AC9E4LY05 Use comprehension strategies to build literal and inferred meaning

Read the passage.

Underline the reason Eagle was surprised that Spider had reached the top of the mountain.

Highlight the clue to how the wind affected Eagle.

"How did you reach this height?" asked Eagle. "You are weak and wingless. Did you somehow manage to crawl all the way up here?"

"No!" laughed Spider. "I simply attached myself to you, and you lifted me from the valleys below on your tail feathers. And I can get along very well without your help too, now that I am way up here. So, Eagle, don't put on any airs with me, because I want to tell you that ..."

Suddenly, a gust of wind swept across the top of the mountain. It slid right by Eagle but it brushed Spider, web and all, back down into the depths of the valley.

Colour words that tell how Spider reached the top of the mountain.

Underline the words that tell what the wind did to Spider.

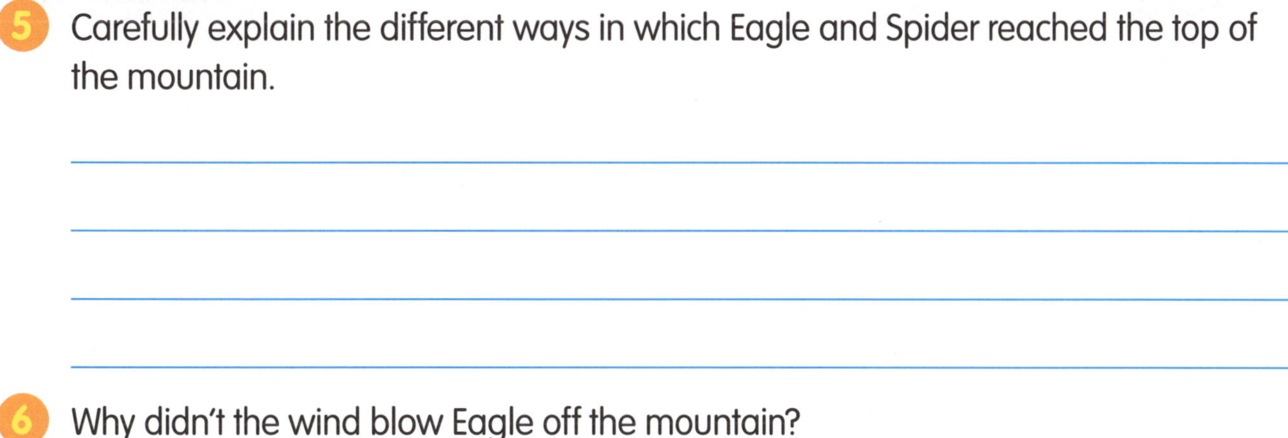

5 Carefully explain the different ways in which Eagle and Spider reached the top of the mountain.

6 Why didn't the wind blow Eagle off the mountain?

7 Why did the wind blow Spider off the mountain?

GRAMMAR LESSON 7

Auxiliary Verbs

Auxiliary verbs help other verbs do their work. They help to show:

- **when** an action happens. For example:
  She <u>is</u> singing. (present) **They <u>were</u> eating**. (past)
  He <u>will</u> run. (future)
- if something is **possible**, **certain** or **necessary**. For example:
  I <u>might</u> go. (possible) **I <u>will</u> go**. (certain)
  You <u>should</u> hurry. (necessary)

Read the extract.

Little Brother

In this sentence, circle the **auxiliary verb**.

"Seriously, Latif," Dara said, "you should sell Little Brother to that man who buys animals for zoos. He will find a good home for him overseas."

In this sentence, colour the **auxiliary verb**.

"Little Brother is not going to a foreign zoo," said Latif. "Little Brother is Malaysian."

In this sentence, put a box around the **auxiliary verb** that helps *think* do its work.

"Then you must think of something," said Dara, as she stacked cups and plates on the table. "If you don't, he might end up like those three wild orang-utans."

"Why can't he go to that orang-utan orphanage you told me about?"

"I don't know where it is."

In this sentence, highlight the **auxiliary verb** that helps *ask* do its work.

"You could ask someone."

"Who?"

Circle the correct answer for each question.

1. *He will find a good home for him overseas.* In this sentence, what is the purpose of the **auxiliary verb** *will*? It helps to show that finding him a good home is …

   a certain. b uncertain. c possible. d necessary.

2. *Then you must think of something.* In this sentence, what is the purpose of the **auxiliary verb** *must*? It helps to show that thinking of something is …

   a certain. b uncertain. c possible. d necessary.

3. *He might end up like those three wild orang-utans.* In this sentence, what is the purpose of the **auxiliary verb** *might*? It helps to show that ending up like the three wild orang-utans is …

   a certain. b uncertain. c possible. d necessary.

AC9E4LA09 Understand past, present and future tenses and their impact on meaning in a sentence

4 Circle the auxiliary verb that correctly completes each sentence.

a	The orang-utan _____ eating a banana.	am	is	are
b	They _____ already adopted an orang-utan.	have	has	were
c	I _____ not see orang-utans when I went to the zoo.	do	does	did
d	Latif _____ already been to the orang-utan orphanage.	have	has	could
e	Latif _____ have to find a new home for Little Brother.	must	can	will

5 Complete each sentence with an auxiliary verb from the box.

am is are was will has does

a Yesterday Latif ____________ paddling his canoe.

b I ____________ try to find a home for Little Brother.

c I ____________ going to the zoo to see the orang-utans.

d The zookeeper ____________ finished feeding the animals.

e Little Brother ____________ climbing onto Latif's shoulders.

f The orang-utans ____________ moving about the enclosure.

g She ____________ not know what happened to the orang-utan.

6 In each sentence, circle the word that is incorrect. Write the correction in the space.

a Dara have washed all the dishes. ____________

b Latif are planning to hide Little Brother. ____________

c The children is playing with the orang-utan. ____________

d Yesterday Dara does not finish all her chores. ____________

e The police does not know who took the animals. ____________

f The orang-utans was swinging from the branches. ____________

g I has just watched a brilliant documentary about apes. ____________

LESSON 136

Engineering Feats

Finding Facts and Information

To find facts and information in a text, we usually ask the questions **Who? What? Where?** or **When?** The answers can be clearly seen in the text.

Read the passage.

Circle the name of the river on which Hoover Dam is built.

Highlight the year in which work on Hoover Dam began.

Colour the year in which Hoover Dam was completed.

Underline the states that Hoover Dam borders.

Put a box around one of the things the water supply from Hoover Dam is used for.

Hoover Dam controls the flow of the Colorado River. It is on the border between the American states of Arizona and Nevada.

Work on the dam began in 1931. Men poured concrete 24 hours a day, seven days a week. The dam was completed in 1935, more than two years ahead of schedule.

Hoover Dam allowed more people to live in America's south-west. The reliable water supply is used for farming. Electricity from the dam's power station is used by people in three states.

Circle the correct answers.

1. **Where** is Hoover Dam? On the border between …
   - a Arkansas and Nevada
   - b Arizona and New Mexico
   - c Arizona and Nebraska
   - d Arizona and Nevada
2. On **which** river is Hoover Dam? On the …
   - a Arizona River
   - b Mississippi River
   - c Colorado River
   - d Snake River
3. **When** was the dam completed?
   - a in 1931
   - b in 1935
   - c in 1924
   - d in 1937
4. **How** many years ahead of schedule was the dam completed?
   - a less than two
   - b exactly two
   - c more than two
   - d three
5. In **what** part of the United States is Hoover Dam? In the …
   - a south-west
   - b west
   - c north-west
   - d south

AC9E4LY05 Use comprehension strategies to build literal meaning

Read the passage.

Underline where you can see the Golden Gate Bridge.

Highlight what kind of bridge the Golden Gate Bridge is.

The Golden Gate Bridge is a suspension bridge across the opening of San Francisco Bay.

Many people said a bridge could not be built there. There are strong currents in the bay, and the water is up to 100 metres deep. It is also a very windy and foggy site.

The Golden Gate was the longest suspension bridge in the world when it was completed in 1937. The bridge's two main cables connect to each end of the bridge and hold up the road. Each one is made of more than 27 000 thinner cables.

Put a box around how deep the bay is.

Circle the date the Golden Gate Bridge was completed.

6 **Where** is the Golden Gate Bridge?

7 **What** kind of bridge is the Golden Gate Bridge?

8 **How** deep is the water in the bay?

9 **When** was the Golden Gate Bridge completed?

10 **What** holds up the road?

LESSON 137

Oceans

Making Connections

Linking a text to other texts you have read is a great way to build understanding. Look for key words and phrases in the texts to make the connections.

Read the passages.

Plants are an essential part of the ocean's food chains. Some sea creatures eat plants. Others are carnivores that eat other sea creatures.

Food chains in the ocean begin with plankton. Plankton is a mixture of tiny animals and algae. Like all plants, the algae use the sun's energy to make food. Very small crustaceans feed on the tiny algae and together they are known as plankton.

Underline the words in each text that tell what plankton is.

Highlight the words in each text that tell how algae make food.

Colour the words in each text that tell what tiny crustaceans feed on.

The word plankton is Greek for wanderer or drifter. It refers to a category of drifting organisms found in the middle and upper levels of the ocean.

Plankton consists of algae, which live near the surface where they can draw on the sun's energy to make food, and tiny crustaceans that feed on the algae.

Small creatures such as krill and shrimps feed on the plankton and larger fish eat the shrimps.

Circle the correct answers.

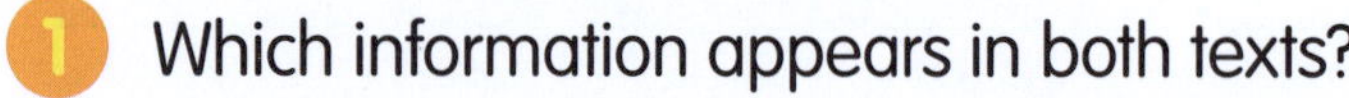

1. Which information appears in both texts?
   - a where the word plankton comes from
   - b what plankton consists of
   - c where algae live
   - d how algae make food
   - e what tiny crustaceans eat
   - f what krill and shrimps eat
   - g what larger fish eat

AC9E4LY05 Use comprehension strategies such as connecting to expand topic knowledge and ideas

Read the passages.

The ocean floor has many of the same features you find on land. Mountain ranges, volcanoes, deep trenches and wide, flat plains are all found on the ocean floor.

When measured from the ocean floor, Hawaii's Mauna Kea rises more than 9 145 metres, making it the tallest mountain on Earth!

Chains of underwater volcanoes, known as seamounts, exist on all ocean floors. Some islands are seamounts that have risen out of the ocean. The Hawaiian Islands are at the end of a chain of underwater volcanoes.

In both texts, underline the things we can expect to see on the ocean floor.

In one of the texts, **highlight** the sentence that shows how little we know about the ocean floor.

In both texts, circle the name of the highest mountain on Earth.

In both texts, **colour** the height of the tallest mountain on Earth.

In one of the texts, **highlight** the name of underwater volcanoes.

The ocean floor is a mysterious world waiting to be explored. We know more about the surface of the moon and our closest planets! What we do know, however, is that the ocean floor has similar features to those found on land, such as mountains, volcanoes and deep trenches.

The tallest mountain in the world actually starts on the ocean floor. It's Mount Kea in Hawaii, which is about 4200 metres above sea level. But below sea level it measures almost 6000 metres, making it slightly higher than Mount Everest.

2 What information do both texts give us about the features found on the ocean floor?

3 What information do both texts give us about the highest mountain in the world?

4 What extra information does one of the texts give us about the Hawaiian Islands?

LESSON 138

To the Limit

Fact or Opinion?

A fact is a statement we can prove is true; for example: A spider has eight legs. An opinion is a statement that expresses a belief or feeling; for example: Spiders are ugly.

Read the passage.

In paragraph 1, underline a statement that we can prove is true.

In paragraph 2, **highlight** the words that express an opinion.

Some people think that plunging down the side of a mountain on a pair of skis is the most exciting feeling in the world. People who do this are called speed skiers. They can reach speeds of 240 kilometres an hour.

It takes cool nerves and topnotch protection to be a speed skier. Rocks, boulders and trees can be deadly so helmets are essential. Avalanches can also be a danger so you need to carry a special light. Then you can be found and dug out of the snow if you are buried by an avalanche.

In 1999, skier Harry Egger of Austria set off down a mountain in France. By the time he reached the bottom, Harry had set a new world record of 248 kilometres per hour. When he got to the bottom of the mountain, he vomited.

In paragraph 1, **colour** a sentence that expresses an opinion.

In paragraph 3, underline three facts.

1 Are the following statements **facts**, or **opinions**? Write **F** next to the facts and **O** next to the opinions.

- **a** Speed skiers reach speeds of 240 kilometres per hour. ______
- **b** It takes cool nerves and topnotch protection to be a speed skier. ______
- **c** Speed skiers carry a special light. ______
- **d** Speed skiers wear helmets. ______
- **e** Some people think that speed skiing is exciting. ______
- **f** Harry Egger comes from Austria. ______
- **g** In 1999, Harry Egger set a new world record for speed skiing. ______
- **h** Harry Egger vomited after setting the world record for speed skiing. ______

AC9E4LY05 Use comprehension strategies to evaluate texts

Read the passage.

Highlight the two sentences that express facts.

Colour the things that can be seen in caves.

Underline the writer's opinion of how caving makes you feel.

Caving takes us deep within the earth. It involves a lot of crawling, squeezing, sliding and stooping, often in mud and water. It is not for people who are claustrophobic or who want to keep their clothes clean.

But caving gives you the most amazing sights: gigantic chambers and deep black holes, underground lakes and rivers, and beautiful stalagmites and stalactites. Perhaps best of all, it makes you feel that you are in a place where no one else has been before.

Circle the word that expresses an opinion about the sights in caves.

Put a box around the word that expresses an opinion about stalagmites and stalactites.

2 In the passage, what **three facts** has the writer given us?

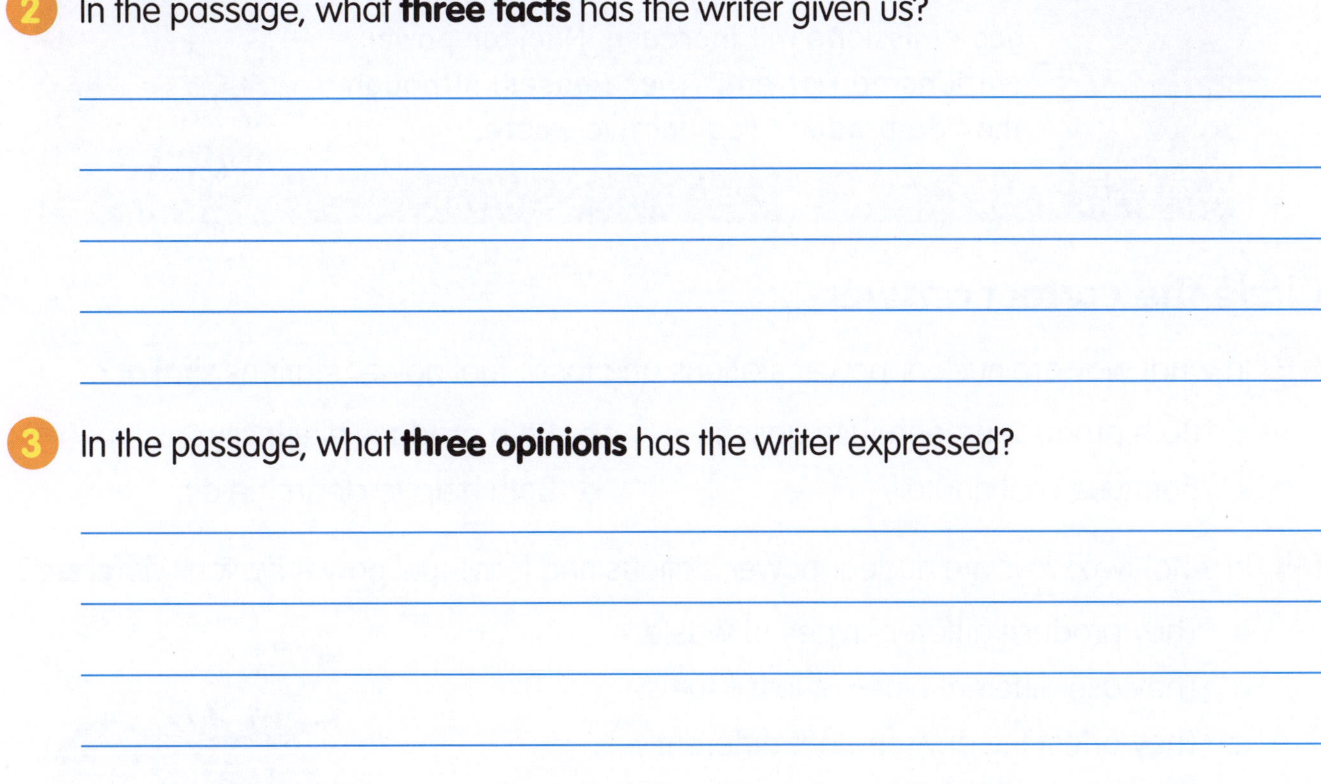

3 In the passage, what **three opinions** has the writer expressed?

LESSON 139

Technological Wonders

Compare and Contrast

When we compare and contrast information, we look for the similarities and differences between details in the text.

Read the passage.

Underline what type of waste fossil-fuel power stations produce.

Highlight what coal and oil are used to produce.

Colour the word that tells what type of fuel coal and oil are.

Nuclear energy is released from the nucleus of a uranium atom, a very dense metal found in the ground. Nuclear energy produces about 10% of the world's electricity.

Supporters of nuclear energy argue that nuclear power stations are safe and much cleaner than fossil fuel power stations. They say there have been very few major accidents in nuclear power stations over 50 years of operation in 30 countries.

More than one-third of human-made greenhouse gases come from fossil-fuel power stations. As people continue to use coal and oil to produce electricity and fuel for transport, the amount of greenhouse gas emissions will increase. Nuclear power stations do not emit these gases, although they do produce radioactive waste.

Put a box around the metal from which nuclear energy is produced.

Circle what nuclear energy is used to produce.

Circle the type of waste nuclear power stations produce.

Circle the correct answers.

1 In what way are nuclear power stations and fossil-fuel power stations **similar**?

a Both produce greenhouse gases.

b Both produce electricity.

c Both use coal and oil.

d Both help to clean the air.

2 In what two ways are nuclear power stations and fossil-fuel power stations **different**?

a They produce different types of waste.

b They use different types of fossil-fuels.

c They affect the environment differently.

d They produce different types of energy.

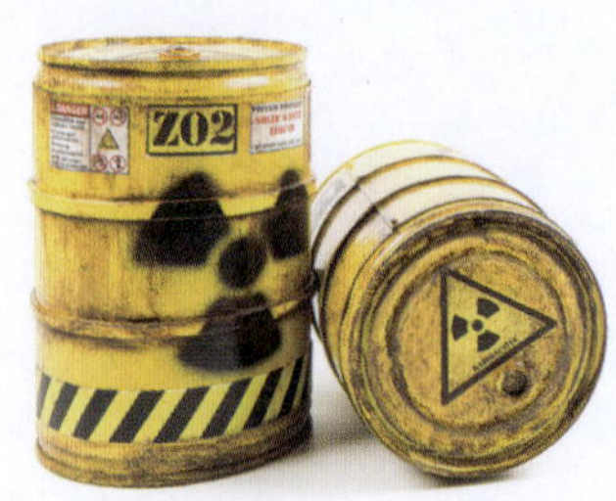

AC9E4LY05 Use comprehension strategies to evaluate texts

Read the passage.

Underline how Charles Lindbergh's flight was different from John Alcock's and Arthur Brown's.

Put a box around the name of the first woman to fly across the Atlantic.

Important Dates in the History of Flight

1903: Orville and Wilbur Wright completed the first flight in an aircraft.

1919: John Alcock and Arthur Brown completed the first non-stop flight across the Atlantic Ocean.

1927: Charles Lindbergh completed the first solo, non-stop flight across the Atlantic Ocean.

1928: Amelia Earhart became the first woman to fly across the Atlantic Ocean.

1961: Yuri Gagarin became the first person to travel in space.

1969: Neil Armstrong and Buzz Aldrin became the first people to walk on the moon.

Colour the name of the ocean Alcock, Brown, Lindbergh and Earhart flew across.

Highlight how Neil Armstrong and Buzz Aldrin's experience in space was different from Yuri Gagarin's.

3 How was the Wright brothers' and Alcock and Brown's experience with flight **similar**?

4 What was **similar** about the flights of Lindbergh and Earhart?

5 What was the main **difference** between the flights of Yuri Gagarin, and Neil Armstrong and Buzz Aldrin?

LESSON 140

Biggest, Highest, Fastest

Drawing Conclusions

To draw conclusions from a text, we have to use clues to make our own judgements. The clues help us find the answers that are hiding in the text.

Read the passage.

Circle how many insects there are for each human.

Highlight the number of new species of insect that are discovered each year.

Put a box around how many locusts there are in a swarm.

Underline how much a locust eats in a day.

Colour the damage locusts can cause.

What makes a small bug big? It's all to do with some very big numbers. Scientists have worked out that there could be 10 quintillion insects alive at any one time. That's 10,000,000,000,000,000,000 bugs or 1.6 billion of them for every one of us. And about 8 000 new kinds are discovered each year.

Some insects, such as locusts, move in huge hungry groups called swarms. Swarms can contain thousands of millions of locusts. To stay alive, every locust needs to eat its own body weight in food each day. A swarm of locusts strips trees bare and gobbles up crops. There is nothing left after a locust swarm has passed.

Circle the correct answers.

1. Which is the best **conclusion?**
   - a Humans outnumber insects.
   - b Insects are big bugs.
   - c Insects outnumber humans.
   - d Insects have long life spans.
2. Which sentence is the best **clue** to question 1's answer?
   - a There are 1.6 billion of them for every one of us.
   - b About 8 000 new kinds are discovered each year.
   - c It's all to do with some very big numbers.
   - d What makes a small bug big?

3. Which is the best **conclusion**? Locusts …
   - a help the environment.
   - b kill insect pests.
   - c weigh a lot.
   - d destroy crops and trees.
4. Which group of words is the best **clue** to question 3's answer?
   - a body weight
   - b hungry groups
   - c nothing left
   - d thousands of millions

AC9E4LY05 Use comprehension strategies to build inferred meaning

Read the passage.

Underline three ways that animals catch their prey.

Highlight the sentence that best sums up the way animals depend on each other for survival.

The slash of a claw, the flick of a tongue, or a strike from out of nowhere can mean life or sudden death.

There's a need for speed in the animal world. All creatures are part of a food chain. The trick here is catching what you like to eat but not getting caught by what likes to eat you.

But fast isn't always about making a quick getaway. To get its food, the hummingbird flaps very fast to stay still!

Put a box around two words that are opposite in meaning.

Circle how a hummingbird uses speed to get its food.

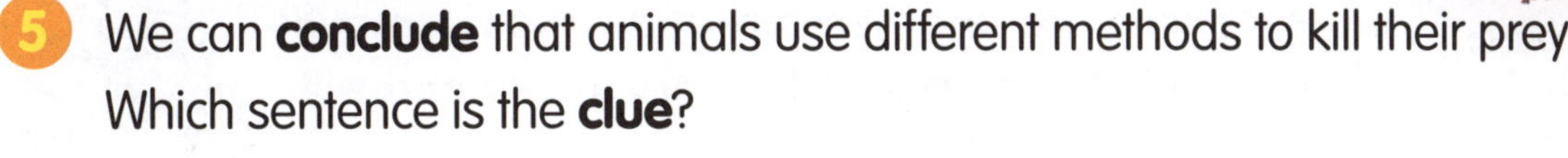

5 We can **conclude** that animals use different methods to kill their prey. Which sentence is the **clue**?

6 Which sentence **suggests** that most animals are both predators and prey?

7 What overall **conclusion** can we draw about survival in the animal kingdom?

GRAMMAR LESSON 8

Plurals and Possessive Nouns

A **plural noun** is usually formed by adding ***s*** to the singular **(dogs, cats)**. A **possessive noun** shows ownership. It is also formed by adding ***s*** to the singular. If there is one owner, there is an **apostrophe (')** before the ***s*** (**the girl's hat**). If there is more than one owner, the apostrophe comes after the ***s*** (**the girls' hats**).

Read the extract.

In paragraph 1, circle all of the **plural nouns**.

In paragraph 2, put a box around the **plural possessive noun**.

In paragraph 2, underline the **plural nouns** that show what the land is being used for.

In the last sentence, **highlight** the **singular possessive noun**.

Here Today, Gone Forever!

Asian elephants are smaller than African elephants. They have small, rounded ears. There are still around 40 000 Asian elephants in the world, but the number is dropping. Scientists think the Asian elephant could soon be extinct in the wild.

Asian elephants are losing their forest homes. Their scrubby forest habitats are being cleared. The land is being used for towns, villages and farms. In Asia, a large number of people live close to the elephants' habitat. Wild Asian elephants often cause damage to these new farms. Sometimes they hurt or kill people. Then these wild elephants are hunted and killed.

Poachers are another threat to these animals. They want the elephant's ivory tusks and will kill the animal to get them.

Circle the correct answer for each question.

In each of the following sentences, identify the plural noun.

1 The Asian elephant has small, rounded ears.

a elephant   b ears   c Asian   d rounded

2 Scientists think the Asian elephant could soon be extinct in the wild.

a elephant   b wild   c extinct   d Scientists

In the following sentence, identify the singular possessive noun.

3 The poachers want the elephant's ivory tusks.

a elephant's   b tusks   c ivory   d poachers

In each of the following sentences, identify the plural possessive noun.

4 The elephants' habitats are slowly disappearing to make way for towns and villages.

a towns   b villages   c elephants'   d habitats

5 The people's farms are close to the forests where the elephants live.

a farms   b elephants   c forests   d people's

AC9E4LY06 Edit written texts for simple punctuation

6 **In each sentence, underline the plural noun and highlight the possessive noun.**

a There were two eggs in the eagle's nest.

b The giant panda's cubs are still very young.

c Poachers took the orang-utan's baby and sold it as a pet.

d Cutting down rainforests has shrunk the tigers' food supply.

e In Africa, humans are clearing land and removing the gorillas' habitat.

f The grey nurse sharks on Australia's east coast are critically endangered.

7 **Circle the word that correctly completes each sentence.**

a The _______ calf is walking beside her. elephants, elephant's, elephants'

b The _______ numbers are starting to increase. tigers, tiger's, tigers'

c Hunting _______ for their meat is now illegal. gorillas, gorilla's, gorillas'

d Beneath its fur, the polar _______ skin is black. bears, bear's, bears'

e Sea _______ lay their eggs on beaches. turtles, turtle's, turtles'

8 **In each sentence, circle the word that is incorrect.**
Write the correction in the space.

a A rhinos horn is worth a lot of money. _______________

b Poachers break the law when they hunt rhinos'. _______________

c The monkey's faces were different shapes. _______________

d The worlds' rainforests are shrinking rapidly. _______________

e Crocodiles' are hunted for their skins. _______________

f A tigers stripes are orange and black. _______________

g Snow leopards' live in the mountains of Central Asia. _______________

ASSESSMENT 4:

What is Pollution?

Lexile: 830

Pollution occurs when rubbish and poisons contaminate the air, water or soil. Pollution is harmful to people, animals and plants. It can cause disease or death.

The air becomes polluted when poisonous gases, dust, chemical fumes and smoke are released into the atmosphere. Burning fossil fuels like coal and oil is a major cause of air pollution. Power stations produce electricity by burning coal. Cars, trucks and buses use fuels that come from oil.

Water becomes polluted when poisons enter our rivers and oceans. These pollutants kill the plants and animals that live in the water. Sometimes the oil from ships and underwater oil wells spills into the sea. The oil floating on top of the water sticks to the feathers of birds and they cannot fly. Fish are unable to breathe beneath the oil-covered water.

Careless dumping of rubbish can cause pollution. Flies breeding in rotting rubbish can spread disease. Animals may become sick from eating the rubbish. They can hurt themselves on sharp objects, wire and broken glass.

The soil can become polluted when farmers use chemicals like pesticides, weed killers and fertilisers on their crops. Animals eating grass grown on polluted land can become sick. Poisons that pass through the food chain can affect people's health.

Noise is another form of pollution. Constant noise can be tiring and stressful. Loud, harsh noises can permanently damage hearing.

Many countries have laws to stop or cut down on pollution. However, we are all responsible for keeping our environment free of pollution.

Circle the correct answer for each question.

1 Which of the following can cause air pollution? **LITERAL**

a spilled oil

b broken glass

c loud noises

d chemical fumes

2 What effect does air pollution have on humans? Air pollution can make humans … INFERENTIAL

a restless.
b sick.
c anxious.
d confused.

3 How do cars, trucks and buses contribute to air pollution? Cars, trucks and buses … INFERENTIAL

a release fumes into the atmosphere.
b churn up lots of dust.
c spill oil on the roads.
d make a lot of noise.

4 Where will pollution from cars be worst? CRITICAL

a in a large city
b in a country town
c on a farm
d on a small island

5 Why are fish unable to breathe if the water is covered in oil? The oil … CRITICAL

a sucks the oxygen out of the water.
b creates too much oxygen in the water.
c prevents oxygen from entering the water.
d causes the water to evaporate.

6 How are air and water pollution similar? Both … INFERENTIAL

a can make people sick.
b are caused by dirty soil.
c are caused by dust.
d are caused by oil spills.

7 Which insects breed in rotting rubbish? LITERAL

a bees
b flies
c mosquitoes
d moths

8 Why do farmers use fertilisers on their crops? CRITICAL

a to destroy weeds
b to remove nutrients from the soil
c to boost plant growth
d to destroy pests

9 Which sentence is true? LITERAL

a Air pollution is worse than water pollution.
b Oil does not harm the environment.
c Air pollution does not affect animals.
d All pollution is harmful.

10 How can people who work in noisy places protect their hearing? CRITICAL

___

___

ANSWERS • PAGES 2–13

Lesson 101

Pg 2

Lots of children heard about the goats and came to visit. Morecambe and Wise put their heads down and butted them in all directions.

The children thought it was great fun—that is, the ones that got away did. The children who didn't escape went home crying and told their mothers.

Mr Kent smiled when he saw what was happening. "These goats are as good as a watchdog," he said. "This'll put a stop to whoever is nicking our strawberries."

Mr Kent wasn't so happy the next day.

He was at the dam. He leaned forward, then called excitedly to Mrs Kent, "We've got some baby yabbies! Hurray!"

1 Teacher check **2** Teacher check

Pg 3

When Mrs Kent went in to wake the children, she was terribly shocked.

"The children aren't here!" she cried to Mr Kent. "Where could they be?"

Mr and Mrs Kent looked everywhere. They looked inside the house and outside the house.

Morecambe started butting his head against Mr Kent as he searched near the shed.

Wise started pushing against Mrs Kent while she peered under the car.

"The goats are trying to tell us something," said Mr Kent.

"Let's untie them and see what they do," replied Mrs Kent.

3 Teacher check **4** Teacher check

Lesson 102

Pg 4

Tessa's Great Grandma Em had a face like a sheet of scrunched up newspaper. Great Grandpop Alfred teased her lots.

"You look like a hippopotamus that has been bathing in the river too long," he said at breakfast.

"The bags under your eyes could carry the treasure from a sunken pirate ship," he said at lunch.

1 d **2** b **3** c **4** a **5** c

Pg 5

By the time the big day arrived, Great Gran's skin was as smooth as whipped cream, her cheeks were as rosy as ripe strawberries, and her eyes were like rich dark chocolate drops.

"You're as lovely as the day I first saw you running across the paddock from the Maloney's prize bull," said Great Grandpop as he waltzed her around the living room.

6 Teacher check **7** Teacher check
8 Teacher check **9** Teacher check

Lesson 103

Pg 6

Anita unfolded a map of Japan.

"It says the capital of Japan is Tokyo. That's where we're going." She read on, "Japan is made up of four main islands and over 3000 little ones." Anita marked Tokyo, on the island of Honshu, with a red spot.

In the corner of the map Jason pointed to a white flag with a red circle in the middle. "That's the Japanese flag," he said. "The word Japan actually means *source of the sun*."

Japan is a country in the Pacific Ocean. It consists of four main islands and thousands of smaller ones. The capital city, Tokyo, is on the island of Honshu.

Japan is known as the *Land of the Rising Sun*. This is because its name means *sun origin*.

Japan is on the Pacific Ring of Fire. It experiences over 1500 earthquakes every year. In 2011, a huge earthquake and tsunami caused a lot of damage.

1 a, b, d, h

Pg 7

Jason looked out the train window. Beyond the rice fields he could see a huge snow-capped mountain. "That mountain looks like an old volcano."

"It is. Japan is full of volcanoes," said Toshi. "That's Mount Fuji, Japan's most famous mountain."

Jason pulled an instant camera out of their bag and took a photo. On the bottom he wrote 'Mount Fuji, JAPAN—famous old volcano.'

Mount Fuji is Japan's highest and most famous mountain. It has been worshipped as a sacred mountain for centuries.

Mount Fuji is an active volcano. It last erupted in 1708.

A good way to view Mount Fuji is from the train on the trip between Tokyo and Osaka. Tourists can often be seen taking photographs of Mount Fuji from the train windows.

2 Mount Fuji is Japan's most famous mountain. It is an old volcano.

3 It is a snow capped mountain and it is the highest in Japan. Mount Fuji has been worshipped as a sacred mountain for centuries. It is still an active volcano and it last erupted in 1708.

4 Teacher check

Lesson 104

Pg 8

Narrator: Long ago in the Dreamtime, Tiddalik the frog woke very thirsty one morning.

Tiddalik: I need water, I need water, I need water ...

Narrator: So Tiddalik drank all the water he could find.

Tiddalik: *[gulp] [gulp] [gulp] [gulp]*

Narrator: He drank so much that every billabong and creek and every river and stream was emptied.

1 d **2** b **3** a

Pg 9

Narrator: Suddenly, Nabunum the eel, whose home had dried out because the water had gone, slithered up to Tiddalik.

Nabunum: Time for you to laugh, froggy.

Narrator: Nabunum began to dance, slowly at first, then faster and faster, wriggling into all sorts of shapes, knots and twists. It worked! Tiddalik started giggling.

Kookaburra: I think he's going to burst.

Wombat: Stand back, here comes the water!

4 Nabunum danced to make Tiddalik laugh.

5 Teacher check

Lesson 105

Pg 10

Long ago, a turtle lived in a pond with two swans. The turtle loved to talk. After a long drought, the pond dried up. The two swans realised they would have to find another pond.

"Don't leave me!" begged the turtle.

"But you can't fly," said the swans. "How can you come with us?" The turtle pleaded and pleaded. The swans at last came up with an idea.

1 b **2** c **3** d **4** c **5** b

Pg 11

When they flew high, the turtle wanted to say "Look at the beautiful view!", but he remembered the swans' warning.

They passed over a small town. People looked up and shouted, "Look at that silly turtle!"

The turtle wanted to cry out, "Mind your own business," but he again remembered the warning. As they flew on, more villagers spotted them. People began pointing and crying, "Crazy swans! Crazy turtle!"

The turtle couldn't stand it any longer. He yelled out, "Go away foolish people!" But he let go of the stick and fell to the ground, landing on his back and cracking his shell into a thousand pieces.

6 "Look at the beautiful view!"

7 over a small town

8 when the people began pointing and crying

9 he fell to the ground, landing on his back and cracking his shell into a thousand pieces

Grammar Lesson 1

Pg 12

Camp Blizzard

Dad asks the service station attendant a quick question and she points in the direction we've just come. Dad hops back into the car with snacks clutched in his hands.

Lucy and I roll our eyes, knowing very well that Dad's navigational skills need work. He has been known to get lost on his way to the local supermarket.

I cheer when I see the Mount Falls National Park sign. Mum stops chewing her fingernails.

"Shouldn't be long now," sighs Dad, as the car rattles and bumps its way over the corrugated road.

The campsite finally comes into view. "There it is!" shouts Dad. "What do you think, Max?"

I'm not sure what to say. My breath is turning to vapour and the chill is starting to creep into my bones.

1 b **2** c **3** a **4** d **5** c

Pg 13

6 **a** her **b** We **c** them **d** our **e** its

7 mine/yours

8 c

9 **a** his **b** it **c** he **d** He **e** he **f** it **g** they

Lesson 106

Pg 14

Most homes received electricity during the early 1900's. Rural homes had to wait longer. Many homes in developing countries still do not have electricity.

Electricity changed the way homes worked. Electric ovens and heaters replaced gas and wood-burning stoves. Electric light bulbs replaced kerosene lamps and gas lights. Electric refrigerators replaced iceboxes. Electricity also led to the invention of the telephone.

1 d **2** a, d, f

Pg 15

The layout of rooms in a home has changed as society has changed.

As plumbing improved, bathrooms became rooms inside the home, rather than outside.

Kitchens only became the centre of homes in the last 60 years. Filled with new appliances, they are no longer hidden rooms used for hard, dirty work. They are linked to open-plan living and dining areas.

Informal living areas at the rear of homes replaced formal living rooms at the front. Living areas were linked to terraces and gardens to create outdoor rooms.

3 The layout of rooms in a home has changed as society has changed.

4 **a** bathrooms became rooms inside the home **b** kitchens moved to the centre and had new appliances **c** living areas moved to the back of homes where they could become linked to terraces and gardens to create outdoor rooms

Lesson 107

Pg 16

Whales, dolphins, seals and sea lions are marine mammals.

Mammals cannot breathe under water because they have lungs, not gills. They must come to the surface to breathe.

The babies of whales and dolphins are born under water. The mothers push the babies to the surface to take their first breath.

Seals and sea lions spend most of their time in the water, feeding on fish, squid and penguins. They also spend time on land, resting. Seal pups are born on land and like all marine mammal babies, they are fed on milk.

1 c, d, f **2** a, d

Pg 17

Many birds depend on the sea for their food. Wading birds, penguins, albatrosses, gulls and pelicans hunt and eat fish and other sea creatures.

Wading birds, such as oystercatchers, live and feed along the shore. Long, spindly legs help them wade through shallow water. Their thin beaks dig around for small animals in the water and mud.

Out over the deeper ocean, birds need to be able to fly for long periods of time. The albatross has very long wings so that it can glide for hours. It can stay in the air for weeks at a time. These seabirds dive into the water to catch their food.

Penguins cannot fly at all. They use their flippers and their webbed feet to swim very fast and catch fish.

3 they both hunt and eat fish and other sea creatures

4 oystercatchers use their thin beaks to dig around for small animals in the water and mud but albatrosses dive into the water to catch food

5 an albatross has long wings so it can glide for hours but a penguin cannot fly at all

Lesson 108

Pg 18

Emperor penguins are the only warm-blooded animals that spend winter in Antarctica.

In May, the female lays a single egg and then walks to the sea to feed. She stays at sea until the egg hatches.

The male stays behind to look after the egg. He balances the egg on his feet and protects it under a thick roll of skin called a brood pouch. During this time, the male does not eat.

The egg hatches after about two months. The chick stays in the brood pouch until it can survive on its own.

The female returns to feed the chick. The male then leaves to find food.

1 c **2** a **3** b

Pg 19

Caribou are wild reindeer. They live in the Arctic regions of Russia, Alaska, Canada and Greenland.

Caribou live in herds. The herd protects calves from predators such as bears, lynxes and golden eagles.

In spring, caribou migrate about 5000 kilometres north to breed on the Arctic tundra. All summer they eat leaves and grass to build up their fat stores for winter.

When the tundra becomes cold and windy, the herds migrate south to the forests. They spend winter in forests, feeding on plants such as lichens and mosses.

4 in spring

5 **a** summer **b** winter **c** the tundra becomes cold and windy **d** winter **e** caribou migrate 5000 kilometres north to breed on the Arctic tundra

Lesson 109

Pg 20

Dear Sir/Madam,

Mr Frame's remark ("That's What Cars Are For", *Tagownda Times*, 12.10.2010) about the role of cars in our community completely misses the point. The debate is about cars picking up and dropping off children outside Tagownda Primary school; it is not an attack on the motor car. The simple question remains: why are so many children arriving at school by car?

The National Children's Nutrition and Activity Survey recently revealed that almost one quarter of children aged two to 16 are overweight. This is a shocking statistic. Encouraging children to walk to school might help to address this major health issue.

1 d **2** b **3** a **4** d

Pg 21

Using cars less often reduces our impact on the environment. Safety is another concern: the more we all walk, the safer our streets become. Tagownda Police Station reports that three accidents involving pedestrians have occurred within half a mile of the front gate of Tagownda Primary school within the last 18 months alone.

As convener of our local "Get Out and About" walking group, I am ready and willing to work with the staff, students and families of Tagownda Primary school to increase the number of students walking to school. In the meantime, we should all be asking ourselves: if it's not hailing, snowing or pouring with rain, how about walking for a change?

Ted Chu

5 uses statistics about the number of pedestrian accidents near Tagowanda Primary school in the last 18 months

6 reduce the impact on the environment

7 he is willing to work with the community to increase the number of students walking to school

8 he uses the pronouns our and I and signs off as Ted Chu

Lesson 110

Pg 22

Glass is made by mixing sand, limestone and soda ash in a furnace. The molten glass is poured into a mould or laid out in sheets. It hardens as it cools.

Glass breaks easily. This property can be changed by adding chemicals or by changing the way glass cools. If you reheat glass, then quickly cool it, the glass becomes much stronger.

Pyrex glass is a special type of glass. It does not expand when it is heated as much as normal glass.

Glass can be recycled over and over again.

1 c **2** b **3** d **4** a **5** a

Pg 23

Most metals come from minerals. Rocks that contain minerals are called ores. They are crushed or heated to collect the metal.

Iron comes from iron ore. It is made into steel by adding carbon.

Metals can corrode. When rust eats away at iron or steel, it corrodes. Rust is a flaky, brown substance that forms when oxygen, water and iron combine. This process is faster if the water is salty.

An alloy is a mixture of metals. For example, stainless steel is an alloy of steel and chromium. Alloys have different properties. They can be stronger, lighter and softer than other metals.

6 crushed and heated

7 because the text tells you rust eats away at iron or steel and that process is faster in salty water

8 because steel is a metal but stainless steel is an alloy and alloys have different properties to pure metals

Grammar Lesson 2

Pg 24

Colonising the World

From the 1400s to the 1700s, many explorers set out from Europe on great sea voyages. These European explorers came from countries like France, Portugal, Spain and Great Britain.

One voyage was led by Lieutenant James Cook. In 1770 he sailed into a bay on the east coast of what would one day be called Australia. He named it Botany Bay and claimed the entire coast for Great Britain.

At the time, there were few jobs in Great Britain. Many people turned to crime just to survive. To ease the pressure on overcrowded jails, Great Britain transported criminals to its colonies in America and later Australia.

In 1787, Governor Arthur Philip left Great Britain for New South Wales with eleven ships. On board were about 1350 people, including 751 convicts. These ships are known as the First Fleet.

1 a **2** b **3** c **4** b

Pg 25

5 a Ocean **b** Lieutenant **c** Endeavour **d** Phillip

6 c

7 a British **b** French **c** Portuguese **d** American

8 a The/Mary Adams/Charles Allen
b Governor Arthur Phillip/British/Sydney Cove
c The Bass Strait/Tasmania/Australian
d The Aboriginal/Australia

Assessment 1

Pg 26–27

1 c **2** c **3** d **4** a **5** c **6** c **7** b **8** c **9** b **10** Teacher check

Lesson 111

Pg 28

I hate being a twin. I guess it might be OK if you were an identical twin. You could fool other people by pretending you were the other twin. But Sam and I only got the bad bits of being a twin—like having to share our birthday. That was a real drag.

"I'm not having a party with all of his friends there," I yelled.

"Now Fairlie," Mum began in her best 'don't-argue-with-me' voice, "I'm not having two separate birthday parties. I don't see why you make so much fuss about this."

1 c **2** b **3** a **4** c **5** d

Pg 29

"Perhaps I should just organise a party for Sam this year," Mum threatened.

"Yeah. Perhaps there should just be a party for Sam," Sam agreed.

"Fine," I said. "Suits me. Sam can have his party this year and I'll have mine next year."

Sam didn't look quite so happy with that idea. Mum did though.

"What a wonderful idea, Fairlie," she said.

"Wonderful," Sam said without enthusiasm.

6 she thought it was a wonderful idea

7 he was happy

8 he wasn't enthusiastic about taking turns

9 the phrase "without enthusiasm"

Lesson 112

Pg 30

Toby climbed down the stairs to the beach. He looked out across the sea as he walked. Suddenly, Toby tripped over something and fell face first into the sand.

Toby stood up and brushed the wet sand from his clothes. He bent down for a closer look at what he had tripped on.

It was a piece of wood. As Toby lifted it, something underneath caught his eye. He dug through the sand and uncovered a bell. Toby lifted the bell and scraped off the barnacles. There was a date carved on its side.

"1892," Toby read.

1 d **2** a **3** b **4** b **5** c

Pg 31

Felix Thompson was seated at the table.

Felix stood and looked at Toby. "I'm sorry about before." Then he handed Toby a black book. "This is my great-grandfather's diary. It tells all about the night of October 12 1892."

Toby was stunned. He opened the lighthouse keeper's diary and read. "It has been a bad week. Storm, after storm, after storm. I was dead on my feet. Fell asleep on watch. The light must have gone out during the night. I didn't know any damage had been done until the next day. When I heard that *The Isabella* was missing in my waters, I lied when I filled in the logbook."

6 he was tired because it had been a bad week of storms

7 a ship called *The Isabella* went missing in the water near his lighthouse

8 he didn't want to get into trouble

Lesson 113

Pg 32

I couldn't believe it. The runway was a lily pad. We were going too fast. How would he stop in time? The lily pad seemed so small. Suddenly, the dragonfly stopped in midair. He hovered over the lily pad and dropped me. Luckily it was a soft landing.

"Do you have any idea how dangerous that is?" I yelled.

The dragonfly said nothing. He flew off, leaving me alone on the lily pad.

A small boat, made from a leaf, pulled up to the side of the lily pad.

"Are you Troy Cooper?" asked the green beetle who was driving the boat.

1 Teacher check

Pg 33

The ants dragged me up the stairs and along a corridor. We came to a door, where another ant was standing guard.

"Is this Troy Cooper?" asked the guard.

"Yes, this is the accused," replied one of my captors.

The door opened. The courtroom was huge. All sorts of insects were seated around the walls. I wished I'd just wake up from this nightmare.

A bee stepped in front of a large platform. "All rise," he buzzed. "I introduce to you, the Honourable Judge William J. Moth."

2 Teacher check

Lesson 114

Pg 34

Two old crows sat on a fence rail,
Two old crows sat on a fence rail,
Thinking of effect and cause,
Of weeds and flowers,
And nature's laws.
One of them muttered, one of them stuttered,
One of them stuttered, one of them muttered.
Each of them thought far more than he uttered.
One crow asked the other crow a riddle.
One crow asked the other crow a riddle:
The muttering crow
Asked the stuttering crow,
"Why does a bee have a sword to his fiddle?"

1 b **2** d **3** a

Pg 35

"Why does a bee have a sword to his fiddle?"
"Bee-cause," said the other crow,
"Bee-cause,
B B B B B B B B B B B B B B B B-cause."
Just then a bee flew close to their rail: -
"Buzzzzzzzzzzzzzzzzzz zzzzzzzzz
zzzzzzzzzzzzzzz ZZZZZZZZ."
And those two black crows
Turned pale,
And away those crows did sail.
Why?
B B B B B B B B B B B B B B B B-cause.
B B B B B B B B B B B B B B B B-cause.
"Buzzzzzzzzzzzzzzzzzz zzzzzzzzz
Zzzzzzzzzzzzzzz ZZZZZZZZ."

4 a rail
b "Buzzzzzzzzzzzzzzzzzz zzzzzzzzz zzzzzzzzzzzzzzz ZZZZZZZZ."
c the two black crows turned pale
d they flew away

Lesson 115

Pg 36

There were once two brothers who were very different from each other. The older brother, though rich, always wanted more. The younger brother was not rich, but he was happy with what he had.

One day the younger brother found a sparrow with a broken wing. He took it home and nursed it back to health. When it was time for the sparrow to fly away, it said, "You showed me great kindness, yet expected nothing in return. Please take this pumpkin seed. Plant it in your garden and wait for it to ripen."

When the pumpkins ripened, they contained gold, silver and diamonds.

1 a **2** c **3** b, d **4** b

Pg 37

News of his brother's sudden fortune reached the older brother. When he heard what had happened, he took out a slingshot, shot a sparrow and broke its wing. He took the bird home and nursed it while thinking, "The sooner you are better, the sooner I get my reward."

When the bird was better, it gave the older brother a pumpkin seed. The seed sprouted into a vine, but the vine did not grow along the ground—it grew up into the sky. "I shall climb the vine and collect my reward," said the older brother.

He climbed the vine all the way to the moon. As soon as he stepped onto the moon, the vine disappeared.

5 he thought once the bird was back to health he would be given a reward

6 Teacher check **7** Teacher check

Grammar Lesson 3

Pg 38

Goat Girl and Garden Boy

Anula was very busy, but she wrote a letter to her mother every week and gave it to Aunty Padma to post. She included a return envelope and stamp each time, but so far her mother had not written back.

Aunty Padma gave Anula money for her school lunches and pocket money for the weekend, but Anula didn't spend the money. She saved it for her bus fare home.

In the meantime, Anula worked hard at her English, music and tennis lessons. She barely had time each evening to slip out of the house with the computer under her arm to visit her pet goat, Beni and her friend, Jegan.

Beni seemed content to remain in Jegan's room—until the day of the Spring Lawn Party. Aunty Padma had planned the party for months. She'd hired a caterer, and she'd invited all the important tea merchants.

1 c **2** b **3** a **4** d

Pg 39

5 a or **b** but **c** so **d** and

6 a Beni had grown bigger/he still fitted in the case.

b Anula was feeling lonely/she wrote to her mother.

c Aunty Padma saw it all/she fainted on the lawn.

d The boy grabbed Beni/dumped him into Anula's arms.

e Anula had enough money for two bus tickets/Jegan could come too.

f Aunty Padma posted Anula's letters home/she kept the ones that came back.

7 A or **B** but **C** so **D** and

Lesson 116

Pg 40

Research stations in Antarctica are busy places. A visitor might describe a typical day like this:

Early this morning I joined a group of meteorologists as they launched a weather balloon. The balloon rose high into the sky and recorded temperature, wind speed and air pressure. Scientists then studied the results.

After that, I watched a glaciologist drill ice cores. Ice cores contain air bubbles of gas from thousands of years ago. Glaciologists studied the ice cores to learn more about the Earth's atmosphere.

1 c **2** b **3** a **4** d **5** b

Pg 41

Research stations in Antarctica are busy places. A visitor might describe a typical afternoon like this:

After lunch, I flew by helicopter to where geologists were collecting rock samples. These contain important information about the Earth from millions of years ago.

Finally, I saw a marine biologist check the electronic tag that was glued to a Weddell seal. These tags record information about where marine animals travel in the ocean.

6 collecting rock samples

7 important information about the Earth from millions of years ago

8 Teacher check

9 Teacher check

Lesson 117

Pg 42

The most common way to make electricity is to burn a fuel, such as coal. This heats water to make steam. The steam spins a turbine. This powers a generator to make electricity.

There are other ways to make electricity. Wind and water can also power a generator. A solar cell absorbs sunlight to make electricity.

Electrical energy can be converted into other forms of energy, such as heat, light and sound.

Lightning is an electrical current that jumps through the air. The current heats the air hotter than the surface of the sun.

1 b **2** b, c, e

Pg 43

Work waiting to be done is potential energy. Work being done is kinetic energy.

Potential energy is energy that could be released or used. A coiled spring has potential energy because the spring could uncoil. A rock on the edge of a cliff has potential energy. Its potential energy is the energy that would be released if it fell from the cliff.

The food we eat becomes potential energy when it is stored in our bodies. When this energy is used to do things, such as kick a ball, it becomes kinetic energy.

3 potential energy

4 Teacher check

Lesson 118

Pg 44

The countries that make up the Arctic often argue about who owns it. Many countries want the Arctic's valuable oil and gas deposits.

In 2007, 50 Russian scientists used a mini submarine to research the seabed under the North Pole. They were trying to prove that the land underneath the Arctic Ocean is connected to their land in Siberia. They even planted a Russian flag on the seabed.

There are over 10 billion barrels of oil and natural gas deposits in the Arctic territory. Canada, Norway and Greenland are also trying to prove that they own the land under the Arctic waters.

1 b **2** d **3** a

Pg 45

An igloo is a dome-shaped shelter, made out of blocks of snow.

What you need:

- A snow saw
- Dry snow

What to do:

1. Use the saw to cut blocks of hard, dry snow, about one metre long and 20 centimetres deep.
2. Draw a circle in the snow and stand in the middle of it. Place the blocks around the circle in layers. The blocks of snow should overlap and lean towards the centre.
3. Place the last block on top of the igloo. Cut it to fit the hole.
4. Cut a tunnel under the wall for the entrance. Poke small breathing holes in the walls.

4 to inform how to make an igloo

5 use, draw, stand, place, cut, poke

6 somebody living in the snow

7 Teacher check

8 Teacher check

Lesson 119

Pg 46

It's summer—let us mow your lawn! Our fast, on time lawn mowing service always does a great job. Long list of happy customers, who enjoy professional work with a smile. Free quotes based on the size of your lawn, how many trees in it and how overgrown it is for the first mow. We also do yard cleanups, weed removal and gutter clearing. No job too big or small.

1 Teacher check

Pg 47

Saturday morning in my house means CARTOONS. Old cartoons, new cartoons, action cartoons, funny cartoons. Cartoon kids, cartoon cats, cartoon squids and cartoon rats. Cartoon goodies being saved, cartoon baddies being blamed. Cartoon wombats in a cage, cartoon aliens in a rage.

But I refuse to watch unless I get my bowl of Corny-Biks. Because cartoons aren't cartoons without Corny-Biks.

2 Teacher check

Lesson 120

Pg 48

Screws hold things together, and lower and raise things.

A screw is an inclined plane wrapped around a cylinder. The inclined plane forms a ridge along the cylinder. This ridge is called the thread of the screw.

As a screw is turned by a screwdriver, it turns a greater distance than it moves forward. The turning motion becomes a forward motion.

A Greek mathematician called Archimedes invented a screw machine more than 1200 years ago. It was used to lift water into fields and out of ships.

1 a, e, f **2** Teacher check

ANSWERS • PAGES 49–61

Pg 49

A wheel with a rod, called an axle, through its centre can lift and move loads.

The axle is joined to the wheel. When either the wheel or axle turns, the other part also turns. The steering wheel in a car is a wheel and axle.

The circle turned by a wheel is much larger than the circle turned by the axle. The longer distance turned by the wheel makes the axle turn more powerfully.

A wheel and axle is often used with gears. A gear is a wheel with cogs around its edge. Several gears can be connected, so that their cogs lock into each other.

3 A wheel with a rod, called an axle, through its centre can lift and move loads.

4 The circle turned by a wheel is much larger than the circle turned by the axle.

5 The steering wheel in a car is a wheel and axle. A wheel and axle is often used with gears.

Grammar Lesson 4

Pg 50

Cold

Some cold habitats have snow and ice all year. Animals have adapted to live in cold habitats.

Many mammals in cold climates have two layers of fur. This keeps them warm and dry.

Some animals hibernate during the winter.

During hibernation, the animal's heart rate and breathing slow down. Their body temperature drops. It takes a long time for the animals to wake up.

Some squirrels, mice, bats and bears hibernate. Before they hibernate, many animals store food as body fat. This fat keeps them alive while they hibernate.

1 d **2** b **3** a **4** d **5** c

Pg 51

6 a the **b** all **c** less **d** a **e** Every **f** That/its/an

7 a an **b** the **c** these **d** more **e** that **f** some

8 A the **B** some **C** Most **D** Many **E** more

Assessment 2

Pg 52–53

1 c **2** b **3** a **4** c **5** c **6** a **7** a **8** b **9** c **10** Teacher check

Lesson 121

Pg 54

Kevin could see the echidna so clearly—its black-tipped, creamy quills, as sharp as knitting needles; the coarse, black hairs on its face, like bristles on a brush; its eyes, two beads shining against the dull blackness of its snout.

1 a, d **2** a, d **3** c **4** d **5** a

Pg 55

Kevin climbed to the highest branch of the tree and balanced there. His legs had turned to stone, but he forced himself to look down. Brown leaves were floating on the murky water, like little boats. He took a deep breath and plunged into the pool. It wasn't the greatest dive he had ever done, but as he surfaced, the fear was gone.

6 metaphor **7** Teacher check

8 Teacher check **9** simile

10 Teacher check

Lesson 122

Pg 56

"If I win the map-a-thon," said Lisa, "I don't want to take Samantha to Wonderland. I want to take Sarah." Sarah is Lisa's best friend.

I couldn't believe that Lisa wouldn't want to take me. She knew how much I wanted to go to Wonderland. I didn't keep it a secret.

"You're the meanest person I know!" I told her. "It would serve you right if someone else won the tickets to Wonderland."

I decided I would do my best to try to win. Then I'd take one of my friends instead of Lisa.

I grabbed her atlas and went to my bedroom to study.

1 c **2** d **3** c **4** a

Pg 57

When Ram saw me, he stopped shouting. I hid behind Buzz, trying to make myself as small as possible.

Ram frowned. He loomed over Buzz. "Do you know the penalty for bringing an outsider into the computer?" he roared.

Buzz nodded. "But I was hoping you would see this as a special case," Buzz said, "and show a little kindness to a poor girl who needs the help of your great, almighty wisdom."

Ram stopped frowning and began to smile a little.

Buzz told Ram about the map-a-thon and the trouble that I'd been having. I needed something to help me remember the names of countries, and cities, and especially of oceans and seas.

5 Teacher check

6 loomed and roared

7 Buzz flattered Ram by talking about his greatness then explained the map-a-thon

8 Teacher check

Lesson 123

Pg 58

At home, Sam looked at the kitchen clock. One hour to go. Part of him was excited but the rest of him was terrified. What if they did something really bad to him? Something where they didn't mean to hurt him, but it went wrong?

Sam knew there was no way out of it. He had to show up. He just wished that Tristan was coming too. He felt rotten about keeping it all from his friend. How was he going to tell Tristan if he did get into the Creaky House Club?

"I'll see you later, Dad," Sam called, as he left the house and cycled towards The Creaky House.

1 b **2** d **3** c **4** c

Pg 59

A voice that sounded familiar said, "Welcome to The Creaky House Club, Sam. As you know, we select our members very carefully. Firstly, we'd like to know why you want to join our club?"

Sam had thought they'd ask him this question, but he still didn't have a good answer.

"Well ... I'm a good basketball player and I'd like to be part of the most popular group in school at the moment," said Sam.

"At the moment?" came the reply. "What do you mean 'at the moment'?"

"I've goofed already," Sam thought. But aloud he said, "Well, at the moment and in the future I mean."

5 The Creaky House Club

6 the dialogue is informal so the text is likely to be a narrative for children aged 8–12 years

7 to entertain young people and spark their imagination

8 Teacher check

Lesson 124

Pg 60

Narrator: Once upon a time, there lived a young woman called Miya. Her father was lord of his people. One day, Miya was swimming in the river when she heard a voice.

Miya: What was that? Who's there?

Narrator: A voice from the sky asked her to follow it through the jungle.

Miya: Sure, I've got some spare time...but as long as I'm home before dark.

Narrator: So Miya followed the voice as best she could through the jungle until she reached a cave.

1 b **2** d **3** a **4** b

Pg 61

Narrator: One day Jose, a farmer from Miya's village, appeared at the cave.

Jose: Miya? Miya? Are you there? There is a famine and we have no food. We are starving. Help us!

Miya: *<to Lord of the Bats>* My husband, I love you but I must leave and return to my village. The villagers need me.

Narrator: So Miya and Jose returned to their village, but Miya did not receive a hero's welcome.

Miya's father: Stop right there! We are hungry because of you, Miya. It is your fault we have no corn.

Narrator: Miya was very upset and returned to the Lord of the Bats.

Lord of the Bats: Don't cry, Miya, because you can still help your village. This is what you must do.

5 Teacher check **6** Teacher check

7 Teacher check

Lesson 125

Pg 62

Lion King wondered which animal could teach the Lion Prince. He wondered if Fox could do it. Fox, though clever, was a great liar and liars always cause trouble. He wondered about Mole. Mole was orderly and careful but never looked far ahead. The King wondered about Panther. Panther was strong, brave and a great fighter but liked fighting a little too much. The Lion knew that a good king is just, wise and can solve things without fighting.

1 a, b, d **2** b, d, f

Pg 63

Lion was still thinking when Eagle flew by. "Of course!" Lion cried. "Eagle!" The Lion King sent his son to study at Eagle's court.

Years later, Lion Prince returned to his father, in time to take over his kingdom.

"Father," said the Lion Prince, "I have learnt many things. I can tell where every bird can find water. I know what kind of food each bird needs. I know how many eggs it lays and the wants of every bird that flies. When I am in charge of the kingdom, I shall begin to teach our animals how to build nests."

The animals in the King's court howled with laughter. The King realised the Lion Prince had not been taught the knowledge a great king needs most of all—a knowledge of the wants and needs of his own people and land.

3 a where every bird can find water
b what kind of food each bird needs
c how many eggs each bird lays
d the wants of every bird that flies

4 the wants and needs of his own people and land, so he could build a strong and happy kingdom

Grammar Lesson 5

Pg 64

How Suan Became Rich

Pedro and Suan were friends. Pedro had inherited a great fortune, but Suan was as poor as the poorest beggar. Early one morning Suan went to his friend and said, "Do you have some wood that you do not need?"

"Yes, I do," said Pedro. He asked his friend what he needed the wood for. Suan replied that he wanted to build a house.

Pedro gave Suan the wood. He told him not to worry about paying for it.

Suan, who had not thought evil of his friend, took the wood and built his house. When it was finished, his house was much better than his friend's house. This made Pedro so angry that he asked Suan to give back the wood

1 b **2** a **3** d **4** c

Pg 65

5 a was **b** wanted **c** did **d** liked
e were **f** would **g** could

6 a needed more bricks.
b was going to buy the house.
c the house was too small.
d would replace all of the wood.
e wanted yellow walls in her room.

Lesson 126

Pg 66

Forces cause earthquakes, wind and waves in and on the Earth.

The Earth's surface is made up of large, slow-moving plates of rock. The plates push against each other and pull apart. This releases energy, which causes the land above the plates to move. This might be an earth tremor that you can't feel or a violent earthquake.

Wind is caused by changes in air pressure. When warm air rises, cooler, heavier air rushes in to fill the space. This moving air is called wind.

Ocean waves are caused by the force of the wind.

1 b **2** c **3** b **4** d

Pg 67

When a basketball player shoots, a push force sends the ball towards the net. Friction with the air slows the ball down. Gravity pulls it back towards the court. The ball would just keep going up without the action of these forces.

An aircraft has four forces acting on it. The engines produce a forward force, called thrust. The wings produce an upward force called lift. Friction from air rushing over the aircraft, called drag, slows it down. Gravity pulls it towards the earth.

What happens to an object depends on the sum of all the forces acting on it. The basketball reaches the net because the force of the shot is greater than the effects of gravity and friction. The aircraft moves forward because the thrust from the engines is greater than gravity and drag.

5 friction

6 gravity pulls both down to Earth

7 a the force of the shot is greater than the effects of gravity and friction
b the thrust from the engines is greater than gravity and drag

Lesson 127

Pg 68

From early times people have set sail on the oceans to explore the unknown. Some explorers looked for new lands to settle. Others looked for fame, treasure or adventure.

Long before science helped us understand the oceans, people thought the Earth was flat. Sailors believed that if they sailed far enough, they would fall off the edge of the world. Of course they never did, but storms, pirates and hidden reefs meant that some ships did sink to the bottom of the sea. Today, adventurers go in search of sunken treasure!

1 c **2** b **3** a **4** d

Pg 69

People have always caught fish and other sea creatures using baskets, hooks and nets. Today large fishing boats can catch, clean and freeze fish while still at sea.

Modern fishing boats take huge amounts of seafood from the sea. Popular ocean fish that people eat include tuna, herring, sardines, cod and snapper. Every year about 75 million tonnes of fish are caught worldwide.

Seaweed is also harvested. People eat it raw or cooked and sometimes use it to thicken foods such as ice-cream and yoghurt. Seaweed can also be used to make toothpaste and sausages!

5 three different methods for catching fish are listed: baskets, hooks, nets

6 the facts about the "huge" amounts of seafood harvested each year: Every year about 75 million tonnes of fish are caught worldwide

7 very useful because versatile

Lesson 128

Pg 70

Many famous buildings become icons. The Sydney Opera House has become an icon of Australia.

In 1955, the State Government decided that Sydney needed an opera house. It wanted one of the world's great buildings, so it ran a competition. There were 233 design entries from 32 countries.

The winner was Jøern Utzon, a Danish architect. He worked with Ove Arup, an English civil engineer. Work began in March 1959 at Bennelong Point on Sydney Harbour.

1 c **2** b **3** c **4** a **5** d

Pg 71

An architect thinks about the land, and where it is, when designing. This is called responding to the site.

Fallingwater is a house famous for the way its design responds to its site. It was designed by an American architect, Frank Lloyd Wright in 1935.

The site was owned by Edgar Kaufmann. It had a stream and a waterfall. Kaufmann thought Wright would design a house with a view of the waterfall. Instead, Wright placed the house right over the waterfall. He told Kaufmann, "I'm designing a building to the music of the stream."

6 the land and where it is

7 Frank Lloyd Wright **8** America

9 Teacher check

Lesson 129

Pg 72

Almost all scientists believe that we should be concerned about global warming. Firstly, they say measurements taken on Earth and in space show that the average temperature is getting higher. They attribute this rise in temperature to the gases released into the atmosphere when fossil fuels are burned.

Secondly, the warmer temperatures are causing vast chunks of ice to melt around the north and south poles, resulting in rising sea levels. This could lead to coastal areas and low-lying land being swamped.

Finally, they point to the shrinking of glaciers in many parts of the world.

1 d **2** b **3** c **4** a

Pg 73

But some people believe that global warming is a natural process that has been happening for the last 6000 years. The average temperature today, they say, is approximately 11 degrees warmer than it was back then, but it has been rising gradually since that time, not suddenly in the last 100 years. These people blame global warming on the way our planets are aligned and the effect they have on our orbit, and that is something we have no control over.

I don't buy those arguments – I believe the science. I have always preferred to err on the side of caution, so I will continue to switch off lights and do whatever I can to reduce my carbon footprint on the planet.

5 It is a natural process that has been occurring over the last 6000 years. They believe it is because of the way the planets are aligned and how that affects Earth's orbit. There are factors outside of our control.

6 the actions like switching off lights will reduce his or her carbon footprint and in time this will help reduce the impact of global warming

Lesson 130

Pg 74

Many reef fish have bright colours. This provides them with good camouflage. Colourful spots and stripes make them difficult to see among the coral. Some fish can even change their colour to hide from predators. Others, such as trumpetfish, are predators that change colour to trick their prey

1 b **2** d **3** a **4** a, c **5** d

Pg 75

Coral reefs are fragile and they need to be protected. There are some natural threats to coral reefs, but people cause the most damage.

Coral needs clear water to grow. When forests are cut down on land, erosion washes soil into the ocean. The plants inside the corals stop growing and the corals begin to die.

Pollution caused by industry and shipping can also poison coral polyps. Ships leak fuel into the water and the boat anchors break off coral. Oil spills can cause huge damage as well.

6 Teacher check **7** Teacher check

Grammar Lesson 6

Pg 76

Saint Patrick's Day

Saint Patrick's Day began as a celebration of an Irish saint. Today it is a celebration of Ireland itself.

More than 1500 years ago, Patrick introduced Christianity to Ireland. He became Ireland's patron saint.

In the seventeenth century, Irish people began celebrating Saint Patrick's Day. Families went to a church service. They also ate a big meal together.

Today Saint Patrick's Day celebrates the history and culture of Ireland. People hold street parades and eat Irish food. They sing and dance to Irish music. Everything is coloured green, the unofficial colour of Ireland.

Saint Patrick's Day is celebrated in more countries than any other national day. In America the Chicago River is dyed green on Saint Patrick's Day.

1 c **2** b **3** a **4** d **5** c

Pg 77

6 a This year **b** On the stage **c** In 1762
d After the Saint Patrick's Day parade
e Before Chinese New Year celebrations begin **f** Every year
g In other parts of the world

7 a After midnight, people set off fireworks.
b In Ireland, Saint Patrick's Day is a public holiday.
c In the northern hemisphere, May Day is a celebration of spring.
d In some countries, May Day has become Labour Day.
e In many countries around the world, Halloween is celebrated on 31 October.

8 Teacher check

Assessment 3

Pg 78–79

1 b **2** d **3** c **4** c **5** c **6** c, d
7 a **8** a **9** b **10** Teacher check

Lesson 131

Pg 80

From now on Sarah's home would be a large, travelling space station. The shuttle was taking them to the big mother ship, Star Wanderer. It would carry all three hundred of them towards Alpha Centauri, and a lifetime of new discoveries.

Suddenly Sarah was scared. It was such an unknown future that lay ahead — like it was for those sailors, hundreds of years ago, sailing over the edge of a flat Earth.

1 Teacher check **2** Teacher check

Pg 81

"We've all left a lot behind us," started Sarah, and many faces grew serious. Dr. Singh was worried. Was Sarah going to remind them too much of earthly celebrations?

"For me, the most important part of Christmas is the Christmas tree. Every year I'd dream about what it would look like. I couldn't wait until it was time to start decorating it." Sarah continued, "Kapil and I have something special that comes from Earth. Something from the past to take us into the future."

Sarah signalled to Kapil, who tugged a cord.

The curtain fell. In front of them was a young apple tree, holding its branches and green leaves high. Seven red apples hung from the branches.

3 Teacher check

Lesson 132

Pg 82

I must be the worst fisherkid on Earth!

It isn't that I don't try. Every chance I get, I'm dangling a line in the water somewhere. My bookshelves are full of every fishing book and fishing map ever printed. I buy the best fishing line pocket money can buy. And I watch all the fishing reports on TV and listen to them on the radio as well.

1 c **2** a **3** c **4** d

Pg 83

The fishing report suddenly becomes very serious. The reporter is warning people about the dangers of fishing from a popular local spot. Two fishermen have gone missing. The camera zooms in on the spot where the fishermen were last seen.

I know the spot — it's called Devil's Rocks. It's a good spot to catch kingfish. Suddenly, a huge wave comes out of nowhere and crashes over the rocky ledge.

5 the reporter says, "a popular local spot"

6 the fishing spot is called Devil's Rocks and during the report a huge wave crashes over the rocky ledge

7 the text says, "the fishing report suddenly becomes serious", and "the camera zooms in"

8 the text says, "a huge wave comes out of nowhere and crashes over the rocky ledge"

Lesson 133

Pg 84

Leaving the brilliant sunshine, it took a while for his eyes to adjust to the inky blackness. The hairs on the back of his neck bristled. Unaware that he was holding his breath, Spook inched forward, his shoes scraping on the earth. His fists were clenched. His fingernails bit into his palms.

The cave was narrow inside. Cobwebs veiled the walls like gauze.

1 c **2** b **3** d **4** a **5** b

Pg 85

Feet barely contacting the ground, the boys bolted — chased by the scream. Spook was in the lead, then Nathan and, well behind, Aaron, his short legs hardly able to keep pace. Branches and thorns stabbed and snatched at them. Long grass tickled their legs like creepy crawlies.

Eventually, out of breath, the trio stopped. They doubled over and gasped for air and their legs ached.

6 bolted

7 Teacher check

8 Teacher check

9 short, raspy, noisy breath that they were unable to make even

Lesson 134

Pg 86

The Opal Miner

In the harsh and brittle desert
In a world of arid air
The rainbow's bending arch
Is magical and rare

1 Teacher check

Pg 87

The Opal Miner

In the tunnels far below it
In a world of stubborn stone
The miner probes and follows
Strange visions of his own.

The miracles he dreams of
Far from dust and heat
Are glowing rainbow fragments
Underneath his feet.

2 Teacher check

Lesson 135

Pg 88

"How lucky am I," said Eagle, "that I have such powers of flight to take me so high and so far. There is no mountain too high for me! Here I am, looking down on all the world from a height no other living creature has ever reached!"

"What a boaster you are," said Spider, from a nearby twig. "Look where I am sitting. It isn't so far below you, is it?" Spider jumped to another twig, just above Eagle's head. He began to busily spin a web, just above Eagle.

"How did you reach this height?" asked Eagle. "You are weak and wingless. Did you somehow manage to crawl all the way up here?"

1 b **2** c **3** a **4** d

Pg 89

"How did you reach this height?" asked Eagle. "You are weak and wingless. Did you somehow manage to crawl all the way up here?"

"No!" laughed Spider. "I simply attached myself to you, and you lifted me from the valleys below on your tail feathers. And I can get along very well without your help too, now that I am way up here. So, Eagle, don't put on any airs with me, because I want to tell you that ..."

Suddenly, a gust of wind swept across the top of the mountain. It slid right by Eagle but it brushed Spider, web and all, back down into the depths of the valley.

5 Eagle flew up to the top of the mountain. Unbeknown to Eagle, Spider attached himself to Eagle, so Spider could reach the top of the mountain.

6 Eagle is heavier than Spider

7 Spider is light and couldn't withstand the higher wind speed at the top of the mountain

Grammar Lesson 7

Pg 90

Little Brother

"Seriously, Latif," Dara said, "you should sell Little Brother to that man who buys animals for zoos. He will find a good home for him overseas."

"Little Brother is not going to a foreign zoo," said Latif. "Little Brother is Malaysian."

"Then you must think of something," said Dara, as she stacked cups and plates on the table. "If you don't, he might end up like those three wild orang-utans."

"Why can't he go to that orang-utan orphanage you told me about?"

"I don't know where it is."

"You could ask someone."

"Who?"

1 a **2** d **3** c

Pg 91

4 a is **b** have **c** did **d** has **e** will

5 a was **b** will **c** am **d** has **e** is/was **f** are **g** does

6 a have/has **b** are/is **c** is/are **d** does/did **e** does/do **f** was/were **g** has/have

Lesson 136

Pg 92

Hoover Dam controls the flow of the Colorado River. It is on the border between the states of Arizona and Nevada.

Work on the dam began in 1931. Men poured concrete 24 hours a day, seven days a week. The dam was completed in 1935, more than two years ahead of schedule.

Hoover Dam allowed more people to live in America's south-west. The reliable water supply is used for farming. Electricity from the dam's power station is used by people in three states.

1 d **2** c **3** b **4** c **5** a

Pg 93

The Golden Gate Bridge is a suspension bridge across the opening of San Francisco Bay.

Many people said a bridge could not be built there. There are strong currents in the bay, and the water is up to 100 metres deep. It is also a very windy and foggy site.

The Golden Gate was the longest suspension bridge in the world when it was completed in 1937. The bridge's two main cables connect to each end of the bridge and hold up the road. Each one is made of more than 27 000 thinner cables.

6 San Francisco Bay

7 suspension bridge

8 100 metres

9 1937

10 the two main cables

Lesson 137

Pg 94

Plants are an essential part of the ocean's food chains. Some sea creatures eat plants. Others are carnivores that eat other sea creatures.

Food chains in the ocean begin with plankton. Plankton is a mixture of tiny animals and algae. Like all plants, the algae use the sun's energy to make food. Very small crustaceans feed on the tiny algae and together they are known as plankton.

The word plankton is Greek for wanderer or drifter. It refers to a category of drifting organisms found in the middle and upper levels of the ocean.

Plankton consists of algae, which live near the surface where they can draw on the sun's energy to make food, and tiny crustaceans that feed on the algae.

Small creatures such as krill and shrimps feed on the plankton and larger fish eat the shrimps.

1 b, d, e

Pg 95

The ocean floor has many of the same features you find on land. Mountain ranges, volcanoes, deep trenches and wide, flat plains are all found on the ocean floor.

When measured from the ocean floor, Hawaii's Mauna Kea rises more than 9 145 metres, making it the tallest mountain on Earth!

Chains of underwater volcanoes, known as seamounts, exist on all ocean floors. Some islands are seamounts that have risen out of the ocean. The Hawaiian Islands are at the end of a chain of underwater volcanoes.

The ocean floor is a mysterious world waiting to be explored. We know more about the surface of the moon and our closest planets! What we do know, however, is that the ocean floor has similar features to those found on land, such as mountains, volcanoes and deep trenches.

The tallest mountain in the world actually starts on the ocean floor. It's Mount Kea in Hawaii, which is about 4200 metres above sea level. But below sea level it measures almost 4800 metres, making it slightly higher than Mount Everest.

2 you can find mountains, volcanoes and deep trenches

3 it is in Hawaii

4 the islands are at the end of a chain of underwater volcanoes, known as a sea mount

Lesson 138

Pg 96

Some people think that plunging down the side of a mountain on a pair of skis is the most exciting feeling in the world. People who do this are called speed skiers. They can reach speeds of 240 kilometres an hour.

It takes cool nerves and topnotch protection to be a speed skier. Rocks, boulders and trees can be deadly so helmets are essential. Avalanches can also be a danger so you need to carry a special light. Then you can be found and dug out of the snow if you are buried by an avalanche.

In 1999, skier Harry Egger of Austria set off down a mountain in France. By the time he reached the bottom, Harry had set a new world record of 248 kilometres per hour. When he got to the bottom of the mountain, he vomited.

1 a F **b** O **c** F **d** F **e** O **f** F **g** F **h** F

Pg 97

Caving takes us deep within the earth. It involves a lot of crawling, squeezing, sliding and stooping, often in mud and water. It is not for people who are claustrophobic or who want to keep their clothes clean.

But caving gives you the most amazing sights: gigantic chambers and deep black holes, underground lakes and rivers, and beautiful stalagmites and stalactites. Perhaps best of all, it makes you feel that you are in a place where no one else has been before.

2 Caving takes you deep into the Earth. Caving requires: crawling, squeezing, sliding and stooping, often in mud and water. Sights you can see: gigantic chambers, deep black holes, underground lakes and rivers, and beautiful stalagmites and stalactites.

3 The sites you see will be amazing. Stalagmites and stalactites are beautiful. Caving makes you feel that you are in a place where no one else has been before.

ANSWERS • PAGES 98–105

Lesson 139

Pg 98

Nuclear energy is released from the nucleus of a uranium atom, a very dense metal found in the ground. Nuclear energy produces more than 16% of the world's electricity.

Supporters of nuclear energy argue that nuclear power stations are safe and much cleaner than fossil fuel power stations. They say there have been very few major accidents in nuclear power stations over 50 years of operation in 30 countries.

More than one-third of human-made greenhouse gases come from fossil-fuel power stations. As people continue to use coal and oil to produce electricity and fuel for transport, the amount of greenhouse gas emissions will increase. Nuclear power stations do not emit these gases, although they do produce radioactive waste.

1 b **2** a, c

Pg 99

Important Dates in the History of Flight

1903: Orville and Wilbur Wright completed the first flight in an aircraft.

1919: John Alcock and Arthur Brown completed the first non-stop flight across the Atlantic Ocean.

1927: Charles Lindbergh completed the first solo, non-stop flight across the Atlantic Ocean.

1928: Amelia Earhart became the first woman to fly across the Atlantic Ocean.

1961: Yuri Gagarin became the first person to travel in space.

1969: Neil Armstrong and Buzz Aldrin became the first people to walk on the moon.

3 they were both firsts for aircrafts

4 both went across the Atlantic Ocean

5 Yuri Gagarin was the first person to travel in space but Armstrong and Aldrin became the first people to walk on the moon

Lesson 140

Pg 100

What makes a small bug big? It's all to do with some very big numbers. Scientists have worked out that there could be 10 quintillion insects alive at any one time. That's 10,000,000,000,000,000,000 bugs or 1.6 billion of them for every one of us. And about 8000 new kinds are discovered each year.

Some insects, such as locusts, move in huge hungry groups called swarms. Swarms can contain thousands of millions of locusts. To stay alive, every locust needs to eat its own body weight in food each day. A swarm of locusts strips trees bare and gobbles up crops. There is nothing left after a locust swarm has passed.

1 c **2** a **3** d **4** c

Pg 101

The slash of a claw, the flick of a tongue, or a strike from out of nowhere can mean life or sudden death.

There's a need for speed in the animal world. All creatures are part of a food chain. The trick here is catching what you like to eat but not getting caught by what likes to eat you.

But fast isn't always about making a quick getaway. To get its food, the hummingbird flaps very fast to stay still!

5 The slash of a claw, the flick of a tongue, or a strike from out of nowhere can mean life or sudden death.

6 All creatures are part of a food chain.

7 Teacher check

Grammar Lesson 8

Pg 102

Here Today, Gone Forever!

Asian elephants are smaller than African elephants. They have small, rounded ears. There are still around 40 000 Asian elephants in the world, but the number is dropping. Scientists think the Asian elephant could soon be extinct in the wild.

Asian elephants are losing their forest homes. Their scrubby forest habitats are being cleared. The land is being used for towns, villages and farms. In Asia, a large number of people live close to the elephants habitat. Wild Asian elephants often cause damage to these new farms. Sometimes they hurt or kill people. Then these wild elephants are hunted and killed.

Poachers are another threat to these animals. They want the elephant's ivory tusks and will kill the animal to get them.

1 b **2** d **3** a **4** c **5** d

Pg 103

6 a eggs/ eagle's
b panda's/cubs
c Poachers/orang-utan's
d rainforests/tigers'
e humans/gorillas'
f grey nurse sharks/Australia's

7 a elephant's **b** tigers' **c** gorillas
d bear's **e** turtles

8 a rhinos/rhino's
b rhinos'/rhinos
c monkey's/monkeys'
d worlds'/world's
e Crocodiles'/Crocodiles
f tigers/tiger's
g leopards'/leopards

Assessment 4

Pg 104–105

1 d **2** b **3** a **4** a **5** c **6** a **7** b
8 d **9** d **10** Teacher check